THE RIDDLES OF ALDHELM

TEXT AND VERSE TRANSLATION
WITH NOTES

BY

JAMES HALL PITMAN

ARCHON BOOKS
1970

[*Yale Studies in English, Vol. 67*]

SBN: 208 00910 8
Library of Congress Catalog Card Number: 75-91189
Printed in the United States of America

AMICO DOCTISSIMO
WILLIAM HAMILTON KIRK

PREFACE

The text of this edition is from *Aldhelmi Opera* (*Monumenta Germaniæ Historica: Auctorum Antiquissimorum Tomus XV*), edited by Dr. Rudolf Ehwald, by whose permission it is here reproduced. I have made no changes but the omission of the *apparatus criticus,* and the substitution of *æ* and *œ* for *ae* and *oe,* and of *u* for the vocalic *v* except in the acrostic and telestich of the *Præfatio*.

To Professor Albert Stanburrough Cook I am deeply grateful for his interest and encouragement during the preparation of the translation, as well as for his painstaking assistance in many matters of detail. My thanks are also due to Miami University, which has defrayed the expense of publication.

Oxford, Ohio, July 1, 1924.

CONTENTS

Contents

The Riddles of Aldhelm

INTRODUCTION

The art of propounding and expounding riddles is as old as literature itself. No people, however primitive, seems to lack them, whether in the form of simple conundrums, or in the more artistic shape of riddle-ballads or riddle-tales; and from all time the ability to solve riddles has been looked upon among simple folk as an indication of wisdom. In higher circles, too, if we may believe tradition, riddles have been in good repute: Solomon is reported as having been expert in the art, and Œdipus saved his life thereby. Hence we find riddles grouping themselves naturally into popular riddles and artistic riddles, though the two classes are, in some measure, mutually interdependent. It is with the latter that we are here concerned.[1]

The father of the modern artistic riddle is Symphosius, a writer so shrouded in obscurity that it has even been contended that he never existed at all. The writer of the riddles, however, whether his name was Symphosius or not, lived probably during the third or fourth century A. D., and was presumably not a Christian, since there is no trace of Christianity in the hundred enigmas by which his name has been preserved.[2] These little three-line poems in correct, though I should say rather prosaic, Latin hexameters are reëchoed in most of the riddles of the Middle Ages. Tupper rightly says: 'The enigmas of Symphosius have dominated all riddles, both artistic and popular, since his day.'[3] The riddles

---

[1] A fine treatment of the general subject of riddles is found in the introduction of Frederick Tupper's edition, *The Riddles of the Exeter Book* (Boston, 1910).

[2] The text of the riddles, with a verse translation, may be had in Elizabeth H. du Bois' edition, *The Hundred Riddles of Symphosius,* Woodstock, Vermont (privately printed by the Elm Tree Press), 1912.

[3] Tupper, *op. cit.,* p. xxx. See also Tupper's paper (*Mod. Phil.* 2 (1904-5). 561-572) on the riddles wrongly attributed to Bede.

The Riddles of Aldhelm

of the Exeter Book in particular owe something to them—
to a certain degree through the medium of Aldhelm, who
was himself the earliest English heir of Symphosius.[1]
Aldhelm (639-709) was the first great English scholar.
He was educated at the school of the Irish monk, Maildulf,
on the site of Malmesbury, and later succeeded his teacher
as the head of the foundation. It was his good fortune at
about the age of thirty-one to become the pupil of the Afri-
can scholar, Hadrian, who came to England in 670; from
Hadrian he must have received most of his really remarkable knowledge of Latin prosody, and of the works of certain
classic writers, together with considerable training in Greek.[2]
Thus Aldhelm was enabled to claim the distinction of being
the first Englishman to write classic Latin verse. His life
was an active and useful one. He founded two new monas-
teries, and at Malmesbury built a new church; and in 705,
when the diocese was divided at the death of the abbot
Hæddi, Bishop of Winchester, Aldhelm was made bishop
of one half, Sherborne, though he still continued to direct
the abbey of Malmesbury.[3]

Aldhelm's principal writings are a lengthy prose work, *De
Virginitate,* a collection of tales which laud the virtue of

---

[1] Aldhelm's indebtedness to Symphosius is remarkably small.
Manitius says (*Gesch. der Lat. Lit. des Mittelalters* 1.137): 'In den
Rätseln ist Aldhelm formal wie inhaltlich von Symphosius und der
Berner Sammlung [see below, p. ix, note 1] abgewichen.'

[2] In regard to the learning of Aldhelm, see Cook, 'The Possible
Begetter of the Old English Beowulf and Widsith' (*Trans. Conn.
Acad. of Arts and Sciences* 25 (1922). 335-9), and 'Aldhelm's Legal
Studies' (*Jour. Eng. and Germ. Phil.* 23 (1924). 105-13).

[3] The principal source for the life of Aldhelm is the fifth book of
William of Malmesbury's *Gesta Pontificum,* which is wholly devoted
to him. This account is based upon sources most of which are now
lost, notably the commonplace book of Alfred. Of modern books
there are such as Browne, *St. Aldhelm: his Life and Times* (1903),
Wildman, *Life of St. Ealdhelm, first Bishop of Sherborne* (1905);
and, better than either, Bönhoff, *Aldhelm von Malmesbury* (1894).

chastity, which he also put into very acceptable hexameters ('well-constructed, and by no means unpoetical,' Ten Brink calls them), and the long and erudite treatise on prosody in which are set his riddles, the *Epistola ad Acircium* (i. e., Aldfrith, King of Northumbria) *de Metris*. In addition to these and some lesser Latin works, he is said to have been a notable poet in the vernacular: according to William of Malmesbury, Alfred considered him the greatest English poet, and from the same source we learn of his making English songs in the manner of a gleeman, and singing them at the bridgehead to the music of a harp, in order to draw people to church. His interest in music[1] as revealed in his writings lends color to this story. By men of his own time he was regarded as a great writer and scholar; Bede speaks of him in the highest terms.

We are here concerned not with the entire *De Metris,*[2] but merely with the hundred riddles contained in it. Ostensibly they are only a group of examples to show what can be done with the hexameter, but actually, that reason is but an excuse for writing a book of riddles on the model of those of Symphosius.[3] Unlike Symphosius, Aldhelm does not limit himself to a set number of lines for each riddle: his poems have from four to eighty-three lines each. Just as in Symphosius, there is a prologue; and the metre is the

[1] Cf. Cook, 'The Old English Andreas and Bishop Acca of Hexham' (*Trans. Conn. Acad. of Arts and Sciences* 26 (1924). 328).

[2] Probably written about 695; see Bönhoff, *op. cit.*, p. 103. On p. 114, Bönhoff further says: '[Die Rätsel] die vielleicht noch früher ein selbständiges Buch bildeten, wie sie denn auch späterhin für sich gesondert wurden.'

[3] Aldhelm clearly acknowledges Symphosius as his inspiration: in the *De Metris* he discusses the 'philosophy' of the riddle, quotes a number of lines from Symphosius, and calls him (*De Metris*, chap. 6; ed. Ehwald, p. 75): 'Simfosius poeta, versificus metricæ artis peritia præditus.' It is possible that Aldhelm knew also a collection of Christian riddles, *Enigmata in Dei Nomine Tullii,* for which see Manitius, *op. cit.*, pp. 136-8, 192-3.

hexameter, which Aldhelm wields with a vigor that, while
the result is scarcely classical, gives his work a real vitality.
'All critics,' says Tupper,[1] 'have noted the larger scale and
freer treatment of Aldhelm's enigmas compared with those
of his model; but, while the writer of Malmesbury has
obviously gained in romantic breadth, he has lost not a little.
Expanding in the joy of creation, he often forgets his riddle's
excuse for being, and lifts the veil of his mystery (Ebert).
Or else he falls into the opposite fault of needlessly com-
plicating and obscuring his meaning. That his contempo-
raries found many lines difficult is shown by the large number
of Latin and English glosses which we meet in the British
Museum manuscripts of his enigmas.' While this statement
is in a measure true, I feel that it does Aldhelm some injus-
tice. He says in his prologue that he means to '*bare* in
speech the secret riddles of created things.' A good riddle
should not be too transparent; but are these true riddles?
Are they not rather an instrument upon which Aldhelm
attempts to play, wishing to reveal, not to hide, the wonder
and mystery of the universe? And herein lies their charm:
to the devout Aldhelm, all things are but outward signs
of their particular portion of the mystery of life. To
an age of exact science, naïve and uncritical wonder at the
boiling of water or the apparently dual nature of the flying-
fish may seem childish; but in so far as we have lost our
impulse to marvel at the truly wonderful, as Aldhelm does,
we are little men, and the apples of knowledge turn to ashes
in our mouths. These riddles often sound ridiculous, or
bombastic, or just dull, but it is seldom that the reader ceases
to feel the force of Aldhelm's underlying purpose—the glori-
fication of God, and the spreading of his kingdom. Far
from being desirous of concealing the subject of each riddle,
he would be defeating his true purpose if he succeeded in
hiding it; hence each riddle is accompanied by its title, so

[1] *Op. cit.*, pp. xxxii-xxxiii.

that there may be no mistake. As for the charge of obscurity, I have found that most of the obscurity is not inherent in the thought, but is rather the result of Aldhelm's delight in employing all the unusual words he can find—airing his vocabulary, of which he is obviously (and pardonably) proud. Most of the difficulties, therefore, melt away before the dictionary, though Aldhelm's carelessness or ignorance in matters of grammar and syntax—notably in the tenses of his verbs—embarrasses one on first acquaintance. As a whole, however, any one who reads the riddles painstakingly is bound to leave them with no small respect for Aldhelm's abilities.

The plan of the work, a certain amount of inspiration, and a few subjects, come from Symphosius; all the rest is Aldhelm's own. He has gathered a store of curious information from a number of sources—Isidore of Seville's *Origines,* for example; and, blending it with many details from his own experience, and from his rather wide reading, he succeeds in making some of his riddles into little poems of real merit, which shed some light on the manifold interests of the man. I have already mentioned his liking for music, shown, for example, in riddle 13, *Organ.* More remarkable is his apparently first-hand knowledge of insects; he has riddles on the silkworm (12; really a moth caterpillar confused by Aldhelm with the silkworm), ant-lion (18), bee (20), locust (34), gadfly (36), water-spider (38), leech (43), and hornet (75), in each of which, while there is usually some literary or legendary material, Aldhelm shows that he has observed the creature. In 75, he even mentions the bitter taste of the 'alimenta' which the hornet provides for its young. For him, all things—animals, plants, stars, natural phenomena, and even furniture and household utensils—speak of the power and wonder of nature and of God; and he concludes with a summary of the whole matter in the last riddle (*Creatura,* 'Nature'), a truly noble poem, full of force and imagination. His worst faults are a desire

to crowd too many ideas into one riddle, and a lust for
synonyms and florid epithets: at times he seems 'word-
intoxicated'. Another is his disregard of the distinctions
between synonyms: for example, in the riddle on the bannock
(70), *clipeus* probably best expresses the kind of shield
Aldhelm means, but he proceeds to use also every other
discoverable word for 'shield' in the Latin tongue. Never-
theless, I am myself disposed to excuse such blemishes in
view of the fertility of his imagination, and his indomitable
enthusiasm.[1]

That these qualities impressed his successors in riddle-
making is evident from the fact that they draw material
from him as often as they do from Symphosius. The much
discussed riddles of the Exeter Book, I am convinced, have
a close connection with Aldhelm's, but, as there are still
differing opinions about this matter, and much acrimonious
ink has been spilled on both sides, I have refrained altogether
from pointing out the relation in my notes, and refer the
reader to Tupper's edition, already mentioned, and to that
of Alfred J. Wyatt,[2] where he will find the evidence well
digested.

The works of Aldhelm have been several times published,
but the best critical edition is the recent one by Ehwald.
The present version is the first attempt at a complete
translation of the riddles, although there are some pleasing
renderings in verse of a number of them in both Browne
and Wildman, and some in prose in Wyatt (including

---

[1] In a suggestive paper, *'Beowulf 1422'* (*MLN.* 39 (1924). 77-82),
Professor Cook points out the very probable influence of Aldhelm's
verse upon the *Beowulf,* which, if accepted, materially affects the
question of the date of the epic. It might here also be remarked
that many things in Aldhelm's poetic style—verse-accent strongly
marked by coïncidence with word-accent, internal rhyme, alliteration.
continual search for synonyms, sometimes resulting almost in ken-
nings—constantly remind one of the similar traits of Old English
verse.

[2] *Old English Riddles,* Boston, 1912.

Creatura (100) complete) and in MacCallum's *Studies in Low German and High German Literature* (London, 1884).[1] My unchanging aim throughout these translations has been absolute fidelity to 'myn auctor', even to the point of trying to make my version dull where Aldhelm is dull, and florid where he is florid. I have endeavored to omit no idea, however slight, expressed in the Latin, and to admit none of my personal flights of fancy—two faults which, I am convinced, lie at the root of most failures in verse translation. It is possible to be just as accurate in verse to the word of the original as in prose, but the task is more arduous; the reward is that verse is more likely to catch the spirit, which so often completely vanishes in prose. Whenever harmony of language has clashed with the sense, I have always preferred accuracy to melody, though it is seldom that, after long enough scrutiny, such problems can not be solved to the improvement of the rendering. If, then, my verses communicate to the reader something of Aldhelm's spirit, along with the substance of his riddles, they will acceptably have served their purpose.

The notes are in no sense intended to be exhaustive, but merely to explain such difficulties as translation alone can not dissipate. In them I am constantly indebted to Ehwald's edition, and thither I refer the reader who desires more extensive comment.

---

[1] Browne, pp. 311-312: Riddles 19, 65, 78.
  Wildman, pp. 83-86: Riddles 8, 21, 25, 33, 40, 66, 80, 87, 92, besides
    Browne's renderings of 19 and 65.
  Wyatt, pp. 84-115: Riddles 16, 29 (lines 4-5), 33, 59, 73 (lines
    4-5), 80, 83, 84 and 100.
  MacCallum, pp. 71, 72: Riddles 19, 30.

It should be remembered that the inaccuracies found in some of these translations are frequently due to the corrupt state of Giles' text.

THE RIDDLES OF ALDHELM

ÆNIGMATA ALDHELMI

Arbiter, æthereo iugiter qui regmine sceptrA
Lucifluumque simul cæli regale tribunaL
Disponis moderans æternis legibus illuD,
(Horrida nam multans torsisti membra VehemotH,
5 Ex alta quondam rueret dum luridus arcE),
Limpida dictanti metrorum carmina præsuL
Munera nunc largire, rudis quo pandere reruM
Versibus enigmata queam clandistina fatV:
Sic, Deus, indignis tua gratis dona rependiS.
10 Castalidas nimphas non clamo cantibus istuC
Examen neque spargebat mihi nectar in orE;
Cynthi sic numquam perlustro cacumina, sed neC
In Parnasso procubui nec somnia vidI.
Nam mihi versificum poterit Deus addere carmeN
15 Inspirans stolidæ pia gratis munera mentI;
Tangit si mentem, mox laudem corda rependunT.
Metrica nam Moysen declarant carmina vateM
Iamdudum cecinisse prisci vexilla tropeI
Late per populos illustria, qua nitidus SoL
20 Lustrat ab oceani iam tollens gurgite cephaL
Et psalmista canens metrorum cantica vocE

THE RIDDLES OF ALDHELM

Prologue

O Ruler, who with thine ethereal sway
Perpetually controll'st the royal throne
Of light, and heavenly sceptre, stablishing
Eternal statutes (yea, Behemoth once
5 Thou punishedst, plaguing his hideous frame
Until he plunged all ghastly from on high),
Patron of him who songs in flowing verse
Composes, now bestow thy gifts on me,
That I with my rude lines may bare in speech
10 The secret riddles of created things—
To the unworthy thus thou giv'st thy gifts.
I summon no Castalian nymphs in song
To aid my task, nor have the honey-bees
Strewn nectar on my lips; I never stray
15 Upon the peaks of Cynthus, nor have lain
On old Parnassus' slope, nor dreamed strange dreams.
For God can fill me with the power of song,
Breathing into my dull mind holy gifts
Of poesy; if he but touch a mind,
20 At once the swelling heart pours out his praise.
Thus lyric measures tell how, long ago,
The prophet Moses sang that bannered host,
Of old victorious, whose fair fame has sped
To every land the bright sun looks upon,
25 Raising his head from out the thundering sea.
And thus the psalmist, lifting up his voice

Natum divino promit generamine numeN
In cælis prius exortum, quam Lucifer orbI
Splendida formatis fudisset lumina sæcliS.

25 Verum si fuerint bene hæc enigmata versV
Explosis penitus nævis et rusticitatE
Ritu dactilico recte decursa nec erroR
Seduxit vana specie molimina mentiS,
Incipiam potiora, sui Deus arida servI,

30 Belligero quondam qui vires tradidit IoB,
Viscera perpetui si roris repleat haustV.
Siccis nam laticum duxisti cautibus amneS
Olim, cum cuneus transgresso marmore rubrO
Desertum penetrat, cecinit quod carmine DaviD.

35 Arce poli, genitor, servas qui sæcula cunctA,
Solvere iam scelerum noxas dignare nefandaS.

INCIPIUNT ENIGMATA EX DIVERSIS RERUM
CREATURIS COMPOSITA.

I. TERRA

Altrix cunctorum, quos mundus gestat, in orbe
Nuncupor (et merito, quia numquam pignora tantum
Improba sic lacerant maternas dente papillas)
Prole vireas æstate, tabescens tempore brumæ.

II. VENTUS

Cernere me nulli possunt nec prendere palmis,
Argutum vocis crepitum cito pando per orbem.
Viribus horrisonis valeo confringere quercus;
Nam superos ego pulso polos et rura peragro.

In measured hymns, reveals the wondrous birth
Of Godhead, born in heaven of God himself,
Begotten ere the Morning Star led forth
30 Those shining orbs that burst upon the world.
But if I versify these riddles well,
Free from all blemish or provincial phrase,
Writing them in correct dactylic verse,
And then if error with its empty show
35 Lead not astray this effort of my mind,
I will begin a worthier task, if God,
Who once did strengthen valiant-minded Job,
Do but refresh his servant's thirsty heart
With a continual dew.   For thou didst lead
40 Cool streams of water from parched, craggy rocks
Long ages past, when Israel's band had crossed
The Red Sea, and attained the wilderness,
As David sang the wonder in his psalm.
O Father, who dost hold the universe
45 Firm in the heavens, deign thou to destroy
The harm and ugly consequence of sin.

HERE BEGIN CERTAIN RIDDLES, COMPOSED ABOUT
VARIOUS CREATED THINGS

1. EARTH

Men call me nurse of all that this world bears,
(And rightly am I named, for never child,
However evil, bites its mother's breast,
And tears it so).   In summer I am green
5 With offspring, but in winter sick and pale.

2. WIND

None can espy me, none lay hands on me;
My rushing voice shrills swift through all the earth.
I shatter oaks with harsh and hideous might,
Yea, beat upon the skies, and sweep the fields.

III. Nubes

Versicolor fugiens cælum terramque relinquo,
Non tellure locus mihi, non in parte polorum est:
Exilium nullus modo tam crudele veretur;
Sed madidis mundum faciam frondescere guttis.

IV. Natura

Crede mihi, res nulla manet sine me moderante
Et frontem faciemque meam lux nulla videbit.
Quis nesciat dicione mea convexa rotari
Alta poli solisque iubar lunæque meatus?

V. Iris

Taumantis proles priscorum famine fingor,
Ast ego prima mei generis rudimenta retexam:
Sole ruber genitus sum partu nubis aquosæ:
Lustro polos passim solos, non scando per austros.

VI. Luna.

Nunc ego cum pelagi fatis communibus insto
Tempora reciprocis convolvens menstrua cyclis:
Ut mihi lucifluæ decrescit gloria formæ,
Sic augmenta latex redundans gurgite perdit.

VII. Fatum

Facundum constat quondam cecinisse poetam:
'Quo Deus et quo dura vocat Fortuna; sequamur!'
Me veteres falso dominam vocitare solebant,
Sceptra regens mundi dum Christi gratia regnet.

3. CLOUD

My color ever changes as I flee,
And leave behind me heaven and earth; no home
Have I upon the earth, nor in the skies.
No mortal fears an exile hard as mine,
5 Yet I with soaking drops make green the world.

4. NATURE (NATURAL FORCE)

Truly, without my guidance naught retains
Its being, yet no eye may see my face.
Who does not know that by my mighty power
The lofty vaults of heaven are rolled around,
5 The sun shines, and the moon pursues her course?

5. RAINBOW

The child of Thaumas was I called of old,
But now I truly tell my origin:
I am the ruddy offspring of the sun,
Born of a watery cloud. At will I haunt
5 The lonely heaven, but shun the southern sky.

6. MOON

Compelled by fates that likewise rule the sea,
I roll out month-long periods of time
In sure-returning cycles. As the light
Of glorious beauty slowly leaves my face,
5 So does the ocean, flowing from the shore,
Lose its increase of waters in the deep.

7. FATE

'T is known that once the sweet-voiced poet sang:
'Whither the God and cruel Fortune call,
Come follow.' Me the ancients falsely named
Mistress, who swayed the sceptre of the world
5 Until the grace of Christ assumed command.

VIII. PLIADES

Nos Athlante satas stolidi dixere priores;
Nam septena cohors est, sed vix cernitur una.
Arce poli gradimur nec non sub Tartara terræ;
Furvis conspicimur tenebris et luce latemus
5 Nomina de verno ducentes tempore prisca.

IX. ADAMAS.

En ego non vereor rigidi discrimina ferri
Flammarum neu torre cremor, sed sanguine capri
Virtus indomiti mollescit dura rigoris.
Sic cruor exsuperat, quem ferrea massa pavescit.

X. MOLOSUS

Sic me iamdudum rerum veneranda potestas
Fecerat, ut domini truculentos persequar hostes;
Rictibus arma gerens bellorum prælia patro
Et tamen infantum fugiens mox verbera vito.

XI. POALUM

Flatibus alternis vescor cum fratre gemello;
Non est vita mihi, cum sint spiracula vitæ.
Ars mea gemmatis dedit ornamenta metallis:
Gratia nulla datur mihi, sed capit alter honorem.

XII. BOMBIX

Annua dum redeunt texendi tempora telas,
Lurida setigeris redundant viscera filis,
Moxque genestarum frondosa cacumina scando,
Ut globulos fabricans tum fati sorte quiescam.

8. PLEIADES

Daughters of rugged Atlas men of old
Have called us; seven are we indeed, though one
Scarce visible. We roam the vaults of heaven,
But also pass beneath grim Tartarus.
5 In blackest darkness we are plainly seen,
But light conceals us. As we first were called,
Our name was taken from the name of spring.

9. DIAMOND

Behold, the impact of unyielding iron
I fear not, nor do burn with heat of flames;
Yet goat's blood softens my unconquered strength,
My natural hardness. Thus blood overcomes
5 One before whom the massy iron quails.

10. DOG

Long since, the holy power that made all things
So made me that my master's dangerous foes
I scatter. Bearing weapons in my jaws,
I soon decide fierce combats; yet I flee
5 Before the lashings of a little child.

11. BELLOWS

My twin and I suck in alternate gusts;
No life have I, yet have the breath of life.
Beauty I give to metals set with gems,
But get no thanks; another takes the praise.

12. SILKWORM

When each year brings the time for weaving cloth,
My livid entrails flow in fibrous threads;
And soon I mount the leafy spikes of broom,
That, fabricating little balls, I there
5 May take the rest ordained me by my fate.

XIII. Barbita

Quamvis ære cavo salpictæ classica clangant
Et citharæ crepitent strepituque tubæ modulentur,
Centenos tamen eructant mea viscera cantus;
Me præsente stupet mox musica chorda fibrarum.

XIV. Pavo

Sum namque excellens specie, mirandus in orbe,
Ossibus ac nervis ac rubro sanguine cretus.
Cum mihi vita comes fuerit, nihil aurea forma
Plus rubet et moriens mea numquam pulpa putrescit.

XV. Salamandra

Ignibus in mediis vivens non sentio flammas,
Sed detrimenta rogi penitus ludibria faxo.
Nec crepitante foco nec scintillante favilla
Ardeo, sed flammæ flagranti torre tepescunt.

XVI. Luligo

Nunc cernenda placent nostræ spectacula vitæ:
Cum grege piscoso scrutor maris æquora squamis,
Cum volucrum turma quoque scando per æthera pennis
Et tamen æthereo non possum vivere flatu.

XVII. Perna

E gemmis nascor per ponti cærula concis
Vellera setigero producens corpore fulva;
En clamidem pepli necnon et pabula pulpæ
Confero: sic duplex fati persolvo tributum.

13. ORGAN

Buglers may blow curved horns of hollow brass,
And harps twang loud, and noisy trumpets blare,
But from my vitals burst a hundred strains;
My mighty voice makes mute the sounding strings.

14. PEACOCK

I am, indeed, surpassing fair to see,
A wonder to the world, yet formed of bone
And sinews and red blood. When life and I
Were fellow-travelers, beauteous ruddy gold
5 Shone not more bright than I, and now in death
Corruption never seizes on my flesh.

15. SALAMANDER

Living in midst of flames, I feel no heat,
And laugh to scorn the dangers of my pyre.
No crackling fire nor glowing ember's spark
Consumes me, for their hot, bright flames grow cool.

16. FLYING-FISH

Now does my wondrous life attract the mind.
I, clothed in scales, with schools of fish explore
The reaches of the sea, or with the birds
Mount through the upper air on soaring wings,
5 And yet I can not live by breathing air.

17. PURPLE-MUSSEL

From twin shells in the blue sea I was born,
And by my hairy body turn soft wool
A tawny-red. Lo, gorgeous robes I give,
And of my flesh provide men food besides:
5 A double tribute thus I pay to Fate.

XVIII. MYRMICOLEON

Dudum compositis ego nomen gesto figuris:
Ut leo, sic formica vocor sermone Pelasgo
Tropica nominibus signans præsagia duplis,
Cum rostris avium nequeam resistere rostro.
Scrutetur sapiens, gemino cur nomine fungar!

XIX. SALIS

Dudum limpha fui squamoso pisce redundans,
Sed natura novo fati discrimine cessit,
Torrida dum calidos patior tormenta per ignes:
Nam cineri facies nivibusque simillima nitet.

XX. APIS

Mirificis formata modis, sine semine creta
Dulcia florigeris onero præcordia prædis;
Arte mea crocea flavescunt fercula regum.
Semper acuta gero crudelis spicula belli
5 Atque carens manibus fabrorum vinco metalla.

XXI. LIMA

Corpore sulcato nec non ferrugine glauca
Sum formata fricans rimis informe metallum.
Auri materias massasque polire sueta
Plano superficiem constans asperrima rerum;
5 Garrio voce carens rauco cum murmure stridens.

XXII. ACALANTIDA

Vox mea diversis variatur pulcra figuris,
Raucisonis numquam modulabor carmina rostris;
Spurca colore tamen, sed non sum spreta canendo:
Sic non cesso canens fato terrente futuro;
5 Nam me bruma fugat, sed mox æstate redibo.

18. ANT-LION

I long have borne a name of hybrid form:
Both ant and lion I am called in Greek—
A double metaphor, foreboding doom:
My beak can not ward off the beaks of birds.
5 Let wise men search out why my names are twain.

19. SALT

Once I was water, full of scaly fish;
But, by a new decision, Fate has changed
My nature: having suffered fiery pangs,
I now gleam white, like ashes or bright snow.

20. BEE

Sprung from no seed, in wondrous manner made,
I bear a burden sweet, from flowers purloined;
My yellow product gilds the food of kings.
Sharp, cruel, warlike darts I ever wear,
5 And, without hands, perform a workman's task.

21. FILE

Bright am I, furrowed, iron-hued, and made
To rub and smooth rough metal with my grooves;
My wont it is to polish massy gold,
And smooth harsh things to perfect evenness.
5 Although I lack a voice, I ceaselessly
Chatter in raucous, ululating shrieks.

22. NIGHTINGALE

My voice is sweet with varying melodies;
I never warble songs with raucous bill.
Though dingy is my color, none may scorn
My singing; and the fear of coming doom
5 Silences not my voice, for winter's cold
May rout me, but with summer I return.

XXIII. TRUTINA.

Nos geminas olim genuit natura sorores,
Quas iugiter rectæ legis censura gubernat;
Temnere personas et ius servare solemus.
Felix in terra fieret mortalibus ævum,
5 Iustitiæ normam si servent more sororum.

XXIV. DRACONTIA

Me caput horrentis fertur genuisse draconis;
Augeo purpureis gemmarum lumina fucis,
Sed mihi non dabitur rigida virtute potestas,
Si prius occumbat squamoso corpore natrix,
5 Quam summo spolier capitis de vertice rubra.

XXV. MAGNES FERRIFER

Vis mihi naturæ dedit, immo creator Olimpi,
Id, quo cuncta carent veteris miracula mundi.
Frigida nam chalibis suspendo metalla per auras:
Vi quadam superans sic ferrea fata revinco;
5 Mox adamante Cypri præsente potentia fraudor.

XXVI. GALLUS

Garrulus in tenebris rutilos cecinisse solebam
Augustæ lucis radios et lumina Phœbi;
Penniger experto populorum nomine fungor.
Arma ferens pedibus belli discrimina faxo
5 Serratas capitis gestans in vertice cristas.

XXVII. COTICULA

Frigidus ex gelido prolatus viscere terræ
Duritiem ferri quadrata fronte polibo
Atque senectutis vereor discrimina numquam,
Mulcifer annorum numerum ni dempserit igne;
5 Mox rigida species mollescit torribus atris.

23. BALANCE

Us nature bore, twin sisters, long ago.
Just, righteous law has ever been our guide;
We disregard the individual right,
To keep the statute. Happy would men be,
5 In this their mortal sphere, if they preserved
The rule of justice as we sisters do.

24. DRAGON-STONE

A bristling dragon's head contrived my birth,
So men report; my crimson hue outshines
Refulgent gems. But never could I get
My proper strength and hardness, if death felled
5 The snake's foul, scaly carcass ere some hand
Wrenched me, all ruddy, from its hideous crest.

25. MAGNET

On me the force of Nature—nay, great God,
Creator of Olympus—has bestowed
This trait, which all the ancient marvels lacked:
I raise cold steel in air, so by strange might
5 Reconquering iron Fate; but adamant
Of Cyprus coming near, I lose my power.

26. COCK

Loquacious in the dark, I ever sing
The ruddy golden rays and noble light
Of Phœbus. I am feathered, and I bear
Among all folk a name of wide repute.
5 With weapons on my feet, I make grim war,
Flaunting a jagged crest upon my head.

27. WHETSTONE

Cold from the earth's chill bowels was I brought.
My foursquare head will smooth down hardest iron;
And I shall never fear vicissitudes
Of age, so long as Mulciber by fire
5 Snatch not away the number of my years:
Grim heat soon softens my unyielding form.

XXVIII. Minotaurus

Sum mihi dissimilis vultu membrisque biformis:
Cornibus armatus, horrendum cetera fingunt
Membra virum; fama clarus per Gnossia rura
Spurius incerto Creta genitore creatus
5 Ex hominis pecudisque simul cognomine dicor.

XXIX. Aqua

Quis non obstupeat nostri spectacula fati,
Dum virtute fero silvarum robora mille,
Ast acus exilis mox tanta gestamina rumpit?
Nam volucres cæli nantesque per æquora pisces
5 Olim sumpserunt ex me primordia vitæ:
Tertia pars mundi mihi constat iure tenenda.

XXX. Elementum

Nos decem et septem genitæ sine voce sorores
Sex alias nothas non dicimus annumerandas.
Nascimur ex ferro rursus ferro moribundæ
Necnon et volucris penna volitantis ad æthram;
5 Terni nos fratres incerta matre crearunt.
Qui cupit instanter sitiens audire docentes,
Tum cito prompta damus rogitanti verba silenter.

XXXI. Ciconia

Candida forma nitens necnon et furva nigrescens
Est mihi, dum varia componor imagine pennæ;
Voce carens tremula nam faxo crepacula rostro.
Quamvis squamigeros discerpam dira colobros,
5 Non mea letiferis turgescunt membra venenis;
Sic teneros pullos prolemque nutrire suesco
Carne venenata tetroque cruore draconum.

28. MINOTAUR

Incongruous is my visage to my frame:
Though horns are on my head, the rest of me
Appears a hideous man; by fame well known
Through all the Gnossian land, a bastard, born
5 In Crete of unknown sire, by double name
Of man and beast together I am called.

29. WATER

Who would not gape before my wondrous lot?
By secret strength a thousand forest oaks
I carry, yet a slender needle breaks
This mighty wain. Yea, all the birds of heaven,
5 And fishes swimming in the flood, from me
Once took their life's beginning. Now I hold
By Nature's law a third of all the earth.

30. ALPHABET

We seventeen sisters, voiceless all, declare
Six others bastards are, and not of us.
Of iron we are born, and find our death
Again by iron; or at times we come
5 From pinion of a lofty-flying bird.
Three brothers got us of an unknown mother.
To him who thirsts for instant counsel, we
In silence quickly bring out hoarded words.

31. STORK

Both shining white am I and dusky black
Together, decked with parti-colored plumes.
No trilling voice is mine, for with my beak
I utter ugly sounds. Though scaly snakes
5 I catch and rend—to them a fearsome foe,
Death-dealing venom never swells my veins;
Nay more, I even feed my fluffy chicks
With poisoned flesh and loathful serpents' blood.

XXXII. Pugillares

Melligeris apibus mea prima processit origo,
Sed pars exterior crescebat cetera silvis;
Calciamenta mihi tradebant tergora dura.
Nunc ferri stimulus faciem proscindit amœnam
5 Flexibus et sulcos obliquat adinstar aratri,
Sed semen segiti de cælo ducitur almum,
Quod largos generat millena fruge maniplos.
Heu! tam sancta seges diris extinguitur armis.

XXXIII. Lorica

Roscida me genuit gelido de viscere tellus;
Non sum setigero lanarum vellere facta,
Licia nulla trahunt nec garrula fila resultant
Nec crocea Seres texunt lanugine vermes
5 Nec radiis carpor duro nec pectine pulsor;
Et tamen en vestis vulgi sermone vocabor.
Spicula non vereor longis exempta faretris.

XXXIV. Locusta

Quamvis agricolis non sim laudabilis hospes,
Fructus agrorum viridi de cespite ruris
Carpo catervatim rodens de stipite libros,
6 Iamdudum celebris spolians Nilotica regna,
7 Quando decem plagas spurca cum gente luebant.
Cor mihi sub genibus: nam constat carcere sæptum;
5 Pectora poplitibus subduntur more rubetæ.

32. WRITING-TABLETS

Of honey-laden bees I first was born,
But in the forest grew my outer coat;
My tough backs came from shoes. An iron point
In artful windings cuts a fair design,
5 And leaves long, twisted furrows, like a plough.
From heaven unto that field is borne the seed
Or nourishment, which brings forth generous sheaves
A thousandfold. Alas, that such a crop,
A holy harvest, falls before grim war.

33. CUIRASS

The dewy earth's cold vitals gave me birth;
I am not made of rough wool, and no loom
Has ever stretched me, nor its humming thread
Leapt back and forth, nor have the Chinese worms
5 Woven me of their saffron floss. By wheels
I was not tortured, nor by carding combs.
Yet, lo, the people christen me 'a coat'.
No arrow in the quiver frightens me.

34. LOCUST

To farmers I am scarce a welcome friend,
For in great troops I raid the countryside,
Eating their crops, and gnaw the inner bark
From tree-trunks. Long ago I gained renown
5 By laying waste the kingdoms of the Nile,
When, for the unclean race, ten plagues they bore.
My heart, imprisoned by my midriff, lies
Below my knees; and there my breast is set,
Beneath my haunches like a squatting toad's.

XXXV. Nycticorax

Duplicat ars geminis mihi nomen rite figuris;
Nam partem tenebræ retinent partemque volucres.
Raro me quisquam cernet sub luce serena,
Quin magis astriferas ego nocte fovebo latebras.
5 Raucisono medium crepitare per æthera suescens
Romuleis scribor biblis, sed voce Pelasga,
Nomine nocturnas dum semper servo tenebras.

XXXVI. Scnifes

Corpore sum gracilis, stimulis armatus acerbis;
Scando catervatim volitans super ardua pennis
Sanguineas sumens prædas mucrone cruento
Quadrupedi parcens nulli; sed spicula trudo
5 Setigeras pecudum stimulans per vulnera pulpas,
Olim famosus vexans Memphitica rura;
Namque toros terebrans taurorum sanguine vescor.

XXXVII. Cancer

Nepa mihi nomen veteres dixere Latini:
Humida spumiferi spatior per litora ponti;
Passibus oceanum retrograda transeo versis:
Et tamen æthereus per me decoratur Olimpus,
5 Dum ruber in cælo bisseno sidere scando;
Ostrea quem metuit duris perterrita saxis.

XXXVIII. Tippula

Pergo super latices plantis suffulta quaternis
Nec tamen in limphas vereor quod mergar aquosas,
Sed pariter terras et flumina calco pedestris;
Nec natura sinit celerem natare per amnem,
5 Pontibus aut ratibus fluvios transire feroces;
Quin potius pedibus gradior super æquora siccis.

35. NIGHT-RAVEN

Man's wit has rightly given me a name
Of twofold sense, for darkness and a bird
Both share it; seldom in the shining light
Of day do I appear; nay, starry shades
5 I rather cherish, and nocturnal dark.
The books that tell of Romulus narrate
How, high in air, I cry with croaking voice;
But in the tongue of Greece my name denotes
That dusky night has ever been my haunt.

36. GADFLY

Though dainty is my shape, keen spurs I wear;
In swarms I wing my way above the peaks.
I get red booty with my reeking blade,
And spare no four-legged beast, but its coarse flesh
5 With goading darts I wound; once fame I won,
Vexing the land of Memphis. Now I pierce
The swelling brawn of bulls, and taste their blood.

37. CRAB

In early Latin, 'Nepa' was my name.
I walk the damp shores of the foamy sea,
And traverse ocean with a backward gait;
Yet airy heaven is by me adorned,
5 Who, ruddy, with twelve stars ascend the skies.
The oyster fears me, daunted by a stone.

38. WATER-SPIDER

My four feet tread the surface of the waves,
Yet not a fear have I of falling in,
But walk on land and water equally.
Nature forbids me swim the rushing stream,
5 Or boisterous rivers cross by bridge or boat;
Rather, I glide dry-foot upon the flood.

XXXIX. Leo

Setiger in silvis armatos dentibus apros
Cornigerosque simul cervos licet ore rudentes
Contero nec parcens ursorum quasso lacertos;
Ora cruenta ferens morsus rictusque luporum
5 Horridus haud vereor regali culmine fretus;
Dormio nam patulis, non claudens lumina, gemmis.

XL. Piper

Sum niger exterius rugoso cortice tectus,
Sed tamen interius candentem gesto medullam.
Dilicias, epulas regum luxusque ciborum,
Ius simul et pulpas battutas condo culinæ:
5 Sed me subnixum nulla virtute videbis,
Viscera ni fuerint nitidis quassata medullis.

XLI. Pulvillus

Nolo fidem frangas, licet irrita dicta putentur,
Credula sed nostris pande præcordia verbis!
Celsior ad superas possum turgescere nubes,
Si caput aufertur mihi toto corpore dempto;
5 At vero capitis si pressus mole gravabor,
Ima petens iugiter minorari parte videbor.

XLII. Strutio

Grandia membra mihi plumescunt corpore denso;
Par color accipitri, sed dispar causa volandi,
Summa dum exiguis non trano per æthera pennis,
Sed potius pedibus spatior per squalida rura
5 Ovorum teretes præbens ad pocula testas;
Africa Pœnorum me fertur gignere tellus.

39. LION

A bristling beast, I roam the wood, and rend,
Although they roar and bellow, tusky boars
And noble, antlered stags; fierce, mighty bears
I pitilessly crunch in gory jaws.
5 I fear no snarling, snapping wolves, myself
A fearsome creature by my royal right.
Wide-eyed I sleep, nor ever close my eyes.

40. PEPPER

Black is my outside, clothed in wrinkled bark,
But inside you will find a snowy pith.
I season dainty food—rich, royal feasts,
And have a place in every soup and stew;
5 But no such virtue will you find in me
Unless you crush my shining inward parts.

41. PILLOW

Now do not disbelieve me, though mine seem
Incredible speech, but open willing ears.
High, towards the clouds of heaven, at times I swell,
And should you take the head, my body too
5 Were gone; but if a heavy head me press,
Deep-sinking, half my bulk I seem to lose.

42. OSTRICH

My heavy body and great limbs sprout plumes;
I have the falcon's hue, but not his flight,
For through the upper air my scanty wings
Could never bear me; rather, I must pace
5 On foot through dirty fields. Smooth eggs I lay,
To make men cups. Phœnician Africa,
So runs the rumor, is my native land.

XLIII. Sanguisuga

Lurida per latices cenosas lustro paludes;
Nam mihi composuit nomen fortuna cruentum,
Rubro dum bibulis vescor de sanguine buccis.
Ossibus et pedibus geminisque carebo lacertis,
5 Corpora vulneribus sed mordeo dira trisulcis
Atque salutiferis sic curam præsto labellis.

XLIV. Ignis

Me pater et mater gelido genuere rigore,
Fomitibus siccis dum mox rudimenta vigebant;
Quorum vi propria fortunam vincere possum,
Cum nil ni latices mea possint vincere fata.
5 Sed saltus, scopulos, stagni ferrique metalla
Comminuens penitus naturæ iura resolvam.
Cum me vita fovet, sum clari sideris instar;
Postmodum et fato victus pice nigrior exsto.

XLV. Fusum

In saltu nascor ramosa fronde virescens,
Sed fortuna meum mutaverat ordine fatum,
Dum veho per collum teretem vertigine molam:
5 Tam longa nullus zona præcingitur heros.
6 Per me fata virum dicunt decernere Parcas;
4 Ex quo conficitur regalis stragula pepli.
7 Frigora dura viros sternant, ni forte resistam.

XLVI. Urtica

Torqueo torquentes, sed nullum torqueo sponte
Lædere nec quemquam volo, ni prius ipse reatum
Contrahat et viridem studeat decerpere caulem.
Fervida mox hominis turgescunt membra nocentis:
5 Vindico sic noxam stimulisque ulciscor acutis.

43. LEECH (BLOOD-SUCKER)

I haunt, all pale, the waters of foul fens;
Fortune has fashioned me a bloody name,
For greedy gulps of red blood are my fare.
No bones, or feet, or arms at all have I,
5 Yet bite with three-forked wounds unlucky men,
And by health-bringing lips thus conquer care.

44. FIRE

Of cold and hardness did my sire and dam
Beget me, but I speedily grew strong
Upon dry tinder; nourished by such food,
I now can conquer fortune, for no thing
5 But water ever can subdue my power.
The wooded uplands, rocks—yea, iron and tin—
I menace, when I loose my natural force.
While life is warm in me, no star of heaven
Outshines me; when at last my race is run,
10 The blackest pitch is not so black as I.

45. SPINDLE

In woodland was I born, a leafy bough,
But Fortune turned my fate another way:
I whirl, and through my smooth neck draw a clew;
No hero wears so long a belt as I.
5 By me, they say, the Fates decree men's lot;
From me is brought the cloth of regal robes.
Cold would destroy men, did not I prevent.

46. NETTLE

Tormentors I torment, but willingly
I none would hurt, unless he first himself
Guiltily sought to pluck my verdant stalk.
The culprit's limbs soon hotly swell; I thus
5 Take vengeance for the wrong by painful stings.

XLVII. Hirundo

Absque cibo plures degebam marcida menses,
Sed sopor et somnus ieiunia longa tulerunt;
Pallida purpureo dum glescunt gramine rura,
Garrula mox crepitat rubicundum carmina guttur.
5 Post teneros fetus et prolem gentis adultam
Sponte mea fugiens umbrosas quæro latebras;
Si vero quisquam pullorum lumina lædat,
Affero compertum medicans cataplasma salutis
Quærens campestrem proprio de nomine florem.

XLVIII. Vertico Poli

Sic me formavit naturæ conditor almus:
Lustro teres tota spatiosis sæcula ciclis;
Latas in gremio portans cum pondere terras
Sic maris undantes cumulos et cærula cludo.
5 Nam nihil in rerum natura tam celer esset,
Quod pedibus pergat, quod pennis æthera tranet,
Accola neu ponti volitans per cærula squamis
Nec rota, per girum quam trudit machina limphæ,
Currere sic posset, ni septem sidera tricent.

XLIX. Lebes

Horrida, curva, capax, patulis fabricata metallis
Pendeo nec cælum tangens terramve profundam,
Ignibus ardescens necnon et gurgite fervens;
Sic geminas vario patior discrimine pugnas,
5 Dum latices limphæ tolero flammasque feroces.

47. SWALLOW

Drooping, I pass long months away from food,
But by deep slumber I endure the fast;
When the dull countryside bursts into bloom,
Its turf red-sprinkled, then my ruddy throat
5 Trills fluent songs. But later, willingly
I flee the tender young and all my race,
And seek the shady coverts. Should some harm
Befall the young chicks' eyes, my secret lore
I wield to cure them, by a healing salve
10 Made of that flower whose name is likewise mine.

48. SPHERE OF THE HEAVENS

The fostering Creator formed me thus:
Smooth round am I, and move in spacious rings
Through all the universe; my bosom bears
The burden of broad lands, and I hold in
5 The swelling billows of the turquoise sea.
Naught in the scheme of things could move so fast,
Whether it go on foot, or wing the air;
No haunter of the sea, whose scale-clad form
Shoots through the green depths, nor the water-wheel
10 That whirls in rapid circles—none of these
Could equal me in swiftness as I turn,
Did not the seven orbs impede my course.

49. CAULDRON

Ugly, capacious, round, of flattened bronze,
I hang suspended, touching neither heaven
Nor lowly earth. I glow with fires, and seethe
With eddying billows; thus a twofold war
5 Of varying risks I bear, as I endure
The limpid waters and ferocious flames.

L. MYRIFYLLON

Prorsus Achivorum lingua pariterque Latina
Mille vocor viridi folium de cespite natum.
Idcirco decies centenum nomen habebo,
Cauliculis florens quoniam sic nulla frutescit
5 Herba per innumeros telluris limite sulcos.

LI. ELIOTROPUS

Sponte mea nascor fecundo cespite vernans;
Fulgida de croceo flavescunt culmina flore.
Occiduo claudor, sic orto sole patesco:
Unde prudentes posuerunt nomina Græci.

LII. CANDELA

Materia duplici palmis plasmabar apertis.
Interiora mihi candescunt: viscera lino
Seu certe gracili iunco spoliata nitescunt;
Sed nunc exterius flavescunt corpora flore,
5 Quæ flammasque focosque laremque vomentia fundunt
Et crebro lacrimæ stillant de frontibus udæ.
Sic tamen horrendas noctis repello latebras;
Reliquias cinerum mox viscera tosta relinquunt.

LIII. ARCTURUS

Sidereis stipor turmis in vertice mundi:
Esseda famoso gesto cognomina vulgo;
In giro volvens iugiter non vergo deorsum,
Cetera ceu properant cælorum lumina ponto.
5 Hac gaza ditor, quoniam sum proximus axi,
Qui Ripheis Scithiæ prælatus montibus errat,
Vergilias numeris æquans in arce polorum;
Pars cuius inferior Stigia Letheaque palude
Fertur et inferni manibus succumbere nigris.

50. MILFOIL (YARROW)

The Greek and Latin tongues both named me thus:
The thousand-leaf, that springs from verdant turf;
My name thus holds ten hundred in its span.
My stalk bears leaves as does no other plant's
5 In all the unnumbered furrows of the earth.

51. HELIOTROPE

Born of my own free will, on fertile sod
I flourish. Yellow flowers adorn my head.
At morn I open, close at setting sun,
And hence the clever Greeks devised my name.

52. CANDLE

Of two materials have open palms
Moulded me. Gleaming white am I within—
My vitals are the shining spoil of flax,
Or slender rush; but all my outer parts
5 Are yellow with a color born of flowers;
They vomit forth hot, fiery flames, and melt,
Dripping a rain of tear-drops from my brows;
Thus I dispel the fearful shades of night.
My vitals burn, and naught but ashes leave.

53. GREAT BEAR

By starry troops encompassed, I am set
Upon the vertex of the world; my name
In common speech is 'wain'. As I revolve
In one continual circle, my swift path
5 I never downward turn, like other stars
That rush from heaven headlong to the sea.
I am enriched by this—that I am near
The axis of the earth, which whirls among
The far Rhiphæan hills of Scythia.
10 In number I am like the Pleiades,
Set in the sky—the sky, whose lower part
Stretches to swampy Styx and Lethe's bank,
Among the black ghosts of the nether world.

LIV. Cocuma Duplex

Credere quis poterit tantis spectacula causis
Temperet et fatis rerum contraria fata?
Ecce larem, laticem quoque gesto in viscere ventris,
Nec tamen undantes vincunt incendia limphæ
5 Ignibus aut atris siccantur flumina fontis,
Fœdera sed pacis sunt flammas inter et undas;
Malleus in primo memet formabat et incus.

LV. Crismal

Alma domus veneror divino munere plena,
Valvas sed nullus reserat nec limina pandit,
Culmina ni fuerint aulis sublata quaternis,
Et licet exterius rutilent de corpore gemmæ,
5 Aurea dum fulvis flavescit bulla metallis,
Sed tamen uberius ditantur viscera crassa
Intus, qua species flagrat pulcherrima Christi:
Candida sanctarum sic floret gloria rerum,
Nec trabis in templo, surgunt nec tecta columnis.

LVI. Castor

Hospes præruptis habitans in margine ripis
Non sum torpescens, oris sed belliger armis,
Quin potius duro vitam sustento labore
Grossaque prosternens mox ligna securibus uncis;
5 Humidus in fundo, tranat qua piscis, aquoso
Sæpe caput proprium tingens in gurgite mergo.
Vulnera fibrarum necnon et lurida tabo
Membra medens pestemque luemque resolvo necantem;
Libris corrosis et cortice vescor amara.

54. DOUBLE COOKING-VESSEL

Who could believe such causes wrought this sight,
Who reconcile such contradictory lots
With common laws of Nature? Lo, I bear
Within my hollow belly fire and flood;
5 Yet billowing water may not quench the flames,
Nor may dire heat dry up the welling streams,
For wave and flame have made a pact of peace.
Hammer and anvil long since shaped me thus.

55. CIBORIUM

I am a house that shelters God's own gift,
And men adore me, but none opens wide
My portals, save by bearing off the roof
Of my four halls; though fiery gems adorn,
5 And ornaments of tawny gold make fair
My body's outward parts, more rich and fine
Are all the parts within, where brightly flames
The beauteous form of Christ; thus holy things
Reveal their glory. Here no timbers are;
10 No columns rise to bear this temple's dome.

56. BEAVER

Upon steep banks along the stream I dwell—
Not slothful, but by weapons of my mouth
Made warlike—and endure a life of toil,
With hook-shaped axes felling heavy trees.
5 Down to the oozy bottom, where the fish
Swim to and fro, I often plunge, and drench
My head in many an eddy. I can cure
Ills of the bowels, heal corrupted limbs,
Dispel the pestilence and deadly plague.
10 For food I gnaw the bitter bark of trees.

LVII. Aquila

'Armiger infausti Iovis et raptor Ganimidis'
Quamquam pellaces cantarent carmine vates,
Non fueram præpes, quo fertur Dardana proles,
Sed magis in summis cicnos agitabo fugaces
5 Arsantesque grues proturbo sub ætheris axe.
Corpora dum senio corrumpit fessa vetustas,
Fontibus in liquidis mergentis membra madescunt;
Post hæc restauror præclaro lumine Phœbi.

LVIII. Vesper Sidus

Tempore de primo noctis mihi nomen adhæsit,
Occiduas mundi complector cardine partes;
Oceano Titan dum corpus tinxerit almum
Et polus in glaucis relabens volvitur undis,
5 Tum sequor, in vitreis recondens lumina campis
Et fortunatus, subito ni tollar ab æthra,
Ut furvas lumen noctis depelleret umbras.

LIX. Penna

Me dudum genuit candens onocrotalus albam,
Gutture qui patulo sorbet de gurgite limphas.
Pergo per albentes directo tramite campos
Candentique viæ vestigia cærula linquo,
5 Lucida nigratis fuscans anfractibus arva.
Nec satis est unum per campos pandere callem,
Semita quin potius milleno tramite tendit,
Quæ non errantes ad cæli culmina vexit.

57. EAGLE

'The squire of unblessed Jupiter, and thief
Of Ganymede,' seductive poets sang.
But I was not that bird who snatched away
The Trojan youth; nay rather, high in air,
5 I scatter fleeing swans, and honking geese
I drive before me through the dome of heaven.
When weary age has bent my senile limbs,
In springs of limpid water then I plunge,
And, dripping, rise restored in Phœbus' light.

58. EVENING STAR (VESPER)

The early hours of night gave me my name;
I haunt the regions where the sloping sky
Bends to the earth; when Titan in the sea
Dips his life-giving body, and the heavens,
5 Changing their course, roll back through crystal waves,
Then do I follow, and conceal my light
Beneath the glassy plain, and happy I
(If I but be not cast down from the heavens)
To quell night's dusky shadows with my gleam.

59. PEN

The shining pelican, whose yawning throat
Gulps down the waters of the sea, long since
Produced me, white as he. Through snowy fields
I keep a straight road, leaving deep-blue tracks
5 Upon the gleaming way, and darkening
The fair champaign with black and tortuous paths;
Yet one way through the plain suffices not,
For with a thousand bypaths runs the road,
And them who stray not from it, leads to heaven.

LX. Monocerus

Collibus in celsis sævi discrimina Martis,
Quamvis venator frustra latrante moloso
Garriat arcister contorquens spicula ferri,
Nil vereor, magnis sed fretus viribus altos
5 Belliger impugnans elefantes vulnere sterno.
Heu! fortuna ferox, quæ me sic arte fefellit,
Dum trucido grandes et virgine vincor inermi!
Nam gremium pandens mox pulchra puerpera prendit
Et voti compos celsam deducit ad urbem.
10 Indidit ex cornu nomen mihi lingua Pelasga;
Sic itidem propria dixerunt voce Latini.

LXI. Pugio

De terræ gremiis formabar primitus arte;
Materia trucibus processit cetera tauris
Aut potius putidis constat fabricata capellis.
Per me multorum clauduntur lumina leto,
5 Qui domini nudus nitor defendere vitam.
Nam domus est constructa mihi de tergore secto
Necnon et tabulis, quas findunt stipite, rasis.

LXII. Famfaluca

De madido nascor rorantibus æthere guttis
Turgida concrescens liquido de flumine lapsu,
Sed me nulla valet manus udo gurgite nantem
Tangere, ni statim rumpantur viscera tactu
5 Et fragilis tenues flatus discedat in auras.
Ante catervatim per limphas duco cohortes,
Dum plures ortu comites potiuntur eodem.

60. UNICORN

Though on the lofty hills the hunter urge
His vainly barking dogs with empty din,
And speed his iron shafts, I fear no risk
Of savage Mars, but, trusting in my might,
5 I boldly set upon tall elephants
And fell them, wounded sore. Yet cruel Fate,
Alas, has tricked me slyly: I who slay
The mighty, by an unarmed girl am caught;
For a fair maiden, laying bare her breast,
10 May take me, doing as she will with me,
And to her high-built city lead me back.
My horn has given me my name in Greek;
Thus, too, the Latins call me in their tongue.

61. DAGGER

First, from earth's bosom was I brought, and shaped
Artfully, while the rest of me was made
From a ferocious bull or fetid goat.
Through me the eyes of many close in death—
5 Through me, who, bare of armor, yet essay
To guard my master's life; my house is built
Of shapen hide and smooth wood split from trees.

62. BUBBLE

In dewy drops I come from rainy skies,
And swell in form by falling with the shower.
No hand may touch me as I float along
Among the eddies, for a single touch
5 Instantly bursts me, and my fragile breath
Into thin air departs. But now I swim,
And lead whole cohorts in my company,
Since many comrades share my origin.

LXIII. Corbus

Dum genus humanum truculenta fluenta necarent
Et nova mortales multarent æquora cunctos
Exceptis raris, gignunt qui semina sæcli,
Primus viventum perdebam fœdera iuris
5 Imperio patris contemnens subdere colla;
Unde puto dudum versu dixisse poetam:
'Abluit in terris, quidquid deliquit in undis.'
Nam sobolem numquam dapibus saturabo ciborum,
Ni prius in pulpis plumas nigrescere cernam.
10 Littera tollatur: post hæc sine prole manebo.

LXIV. Columba

Cum Deus infandas iam plecteret æquore noxas
Ablueretque simul scelerum contagia limphis,
Prima præcepti complevi iussa parentis
Portendens fructu terris venisse salutem.
5 Mitia quapropter semper præcordia gesto
Et felix præpes nigro sine felle manebo.

LXV. Muriceps

Fida satis custos conservans pervigil ædes
Noctibus in furvis cæcas lustrabo latebras
Atris haud perdens oculorum lumen in antris.
Furibus invisis, vastant qui farris acervos,
5 Insidiis tacite dispono scandala mortis.
Et vaga venatrix rimabor lustra ferarum,
Nec volo cum canibus turmas agitare fugaces,
Qui mihi latrantes crudelia bella ciebunt.
Gens exosa mihi tradebat nomen habendum.

63. RAVEN

When ruthless flood slew all the human race,
And new-made oceans punished every soul
Save those few only who bore on the seed
Of this world's life, I, first of living things,
5 Renounced the pact, and would not bend my neck
Beneath the patriarch's rule; whence, as I think,
The poet says: 'On earth it washed away
The sin committed on the rolling flood.'
I never gratify my young with food
10 Until I see their feathers blackening
Beneath the skin. One letter take away,
And barren shall I be of progeny.

64. DOVE

When God by flood was punishing vile sin,
And by those waters cleansing evil's stain,
I first fulfilled the patriarch's command,
As by a fruitful bough I signified
5 Salvation to the earth was come. Thenceforth
My heart is ever gentle, and in me,
A happy bird, no black bile ever flows.

65. CAT

I am the faithful guardian of the house,
And vigilantly keep it all night long,
Roaming among blind shadows, for my eyes
Lose not their light, though in a pitchy cave.
5 In crafty ambush for such cursed thieves
As prey upon the stored-up grain, I set
The silent snares of death, and prying, find
The lair of beasts, a roving huntress I.
Yet will I not pursue the fleeing bands
10 With baying hounds, for dogs would turn on me,
And bark at me their threat of cruel war.
A race I hate has given me my name.

LXVI. MOLA

Nos sumus æquales communi sorte sorores,
Quæ damus ex nostro cunctis alimenta labore.
Par labor ambarum, dispar fortuna duarum;
Altera nam cursat, quod numquam altera gessit;
5 Nec tamen invidiæ stimulis agitamur acerbis:
Utraque, quod mandit, quod ruminat ore patenti,
Comminuens reddit famulans sine fraude maligna.

LXVII. CRIBELLUS

Sicca pruinosam crebris effundo fenestris
Candentemque nivem iactans de viscere furvo;
Et tamen omnis amat, quamvis sit frigida, nimbo
Densior et nebulis late spargatur in aula.
5 Qua sine mortales grassantur funere leti
7 (Sic animæ pariter pereunt, dum vita fatescit)
6 Et qua ditati contemnunt limina Ditis.
Liquitur in prunis numquam torrentibus hæc nix,
Sed, mirum dictu, magis indurescit ad ignem.

LXVIII. SALPIX

Sum cava, bellantum crepitu quæ corda ciebo,
Vocibus horrendis stimulans in bella cohortes.
Idcirco reboans tanto clamore resulto,
Quod nulla interius obtundant viscera vocem;
5 Spiritus in toto sed regnant corpore flabra.
Garrula me poterit numquam superare cicada
Aut arguta simul cantans luscinia ruscis,
Quam lingua propria dicunt acalantida Græci.

66. MILL

Sisters are we, alike in mutual lot,
Who by our toil give food to all mankind.
Our labor equal is, but not our fate:
One runs about, the other never moves,
5 Yet envy's biting stings disturb us not.
Each, crushing into bits what she devours,
Chewing with open mouth, gives back again
What she received, for honest thralls are we.

67. SIEVE

Though dry, from countless windows I pour out
Hoar frost and gleaming snow, from dark insides
Tossing it down. Yet mortals cherish it,
Though it be cold, and sprinkled in the hall
5 Thicker than mist or rain. Men, lacking it,
Wander about, a pageantry of death
(Thus wanes our breath, as strength of life decays),
But its possessors scorn the gates of Dis.
In glowing coals this snow will never melt;
10 Nay, fire miraculously hardens it.

68. TRUMPET

Hollow am I, and stir the warrior's heart
With bellowing, urging cohorts on to war
By horrid utterance. Thus resounding loud,
With greater clamor I reverberate
5 Because in me no vitals dull my voice;
For windy gusts of breath my body fill.
Never can chirping locust drown me out,
Nor nightingale that sings among the broom—
The bird called 'acalanthis' by the Greeks.

LXIX. Taxus

Semper habens virides frondenti in corpore crines
Tempore non ullo viduabor tegmine spisso,
Circius et Boreas quamvis et flamina Chauri
Viribus horrendis studeant deglobere frontem;
5 Sed me pestiferam fecerunt fata reorum,
Cumque venenatus glescit de corpore stipes,
Lurcones rabidi quem carpunt rictibus oris,
Occido mandentum mox plura cadavera leto.

LXX. Tortella

De terris orior candenti corpore pelta
Et nive fecunda, Vulcani torre rigescens,
Carior et multo quam cetera scuta duelli;
Nec tamen in medio clipei stat ferreus umbo.
5 Me sine quid prodest dirorum parma virorum?
Vix artus animæque carerent tramite mortis,
Ni forsan validis refrager viribus Orco.

LXXI. Piscis

Me pedibus manibusque simul fraudaverat almus
Arbiter, immensum primo dum pangeret orbem.
Fulcior haud volitans veloci præpetis ala
Spiritus alterno vegitat nec corpora flatu.
5 Quamvis in cælis convexa cacumina cernam,
Non tamen undosi contemno marmora ponti.

69. YEW-TREE

With verdant locks my leafy form is crowned,
A thick-grown covering I shall never lack,
Though Boreas and all the windy gusts
Of North and West exert their hideous strength
5 To bare my brow. But Fate, that rules all things,
Made me pestiferous: from me there grow
Poisonous branches, which when gluttons eat,
Mad in their greediness, with yawning mouths,
Many the corpses that I fell in death.

70. BANNOCK

From earth I rise, a shield of shining white,
Made of life-giving snow grown hard in fire;
Far dearer am I than those other shields
That men in battle use, yet on this targe
5 There stands no boss of iron. Lacking me,
What can the bucklers of grim heroes do?
Scarce would a soul escape the Stygian way,
If I with sturdy strength opposed not death.

71. FISH

The Lord Creator both of feet and hands
Defrauded me, when first he set in place
The world immeasurable. I do not fly,
Borne on the pinions of a bird; no breath
5 Livens my body with recurrent gusts.
I may behold the vaulted arch of heaven,
Yet scorn not rolling ocean's broad expanse.

LXXII. Colosus

Omnia membra mihi plasmavit corporis auctor,
Nec tamen ex isdem membrorum munia sumpsi,
Pergere nec plantis oculis nec cernere possum,
Quamquam nunc patulæ constent sub fronte fenestræ.
5 Nullus anhelanti procedit viscere flatus
Spicula nec geminis nitor torquere lacertis.
Heu! frustra factor confinxit corpus inorme,
Totis membrorum dum frauder sensibus intus.

LXXIII. Fons

Per cava telluris clam serpo celerrimus antra
Flexos venarum girans anfractibus orbes;
Cum caream vita sensu quoque funditus expers,
Quis numerus capiat vel quis laterculus æquet,
5 Vita viventum generem quot milia partu?
His neque per cælum rutilantis sidera speræ
Fluctivagi ponti nec compensantur harenæ.

LXXIV. Fundibalum

Glauca seges lini vernans ex æquore campi
Et tergus mihi tradebant primordia fati.
Bina mihi constant torto retinacula filo,
Ex quibus immensum trucidabam mole tirannum,
5 Cum cuperent olim gentis sævire falanges.
Plus amo cum tereti bellum decernere saxo
Quam duris pugnans ferrata cuspide contis.
Tres digiti totum versant super ardua corpus;
Erro caput circa tenues et tendor in auras.

72. Colossus

My body's maker moulded all my parts,
Yet I no service from my members get:
On feet I walk not, nor can see with eyes,
Though open windows stand beneath my brows;
5 No breath proceeds from out my panting lungs,
Nor do my two arms strive to cast their darts.
Alas! in vain my maker fashioned me
A form enormous, since within that form
I lack all feeling in my various parts.

73. Spring of Water

In hollow caverns of the earth I wind
My swift and secret way, through tortuous veins
Twisting in bending circles; though I lack
Life and sensation, I am skilled in this.
5 What number can express, what census tell,
The myriad living creatures I produce?
Not all the stars set in the flashing sphere
Rolling through heaven in number equal them,
Nor all the sands beneath the restless sea.

74. Sling

The flax-plant, blooming fair in level fields,
And a bull's hide, gave me my origin.
Two bonds of twisted cord restrain my leap,
And thus long since I slaughtered with a weight
5 A mighty tyrant, when the marshaled host
Was bent on cruel war; for I prefer
To win my battles with a smooth, round stone
Rather than with hard iron-headed pikes.
Three fingers whirl me high about the head;
10 I turn, and dart away into thin air.

LXXV. CRABRO

Aëra per sudum nunc binis remigo pennis
Horridus et grossæ depromo murmura vocis
Inque cavo densis conversor stipite turmis
Dulcia conficiens propriis alimenta catervis,
5 Et tamen humanis horrent hæc pabula buccis.
Sed quicumque cupit disrumpens fœdera pacis
Dirus commaculare domum sub culmine querno,
Extemplo socias in bellum clamo cohortes,
Dumque catervatim stridunt et spicula trudunt,
10 Agmina defugiunt iaculis exterrita diris:
Insontes hosti sic torquent tela nocenti
Plurima, quæ constant tetris infecta venenis.

LXXVI. MELARIUS

Fausta fuit primo mundi nascentis origo,
Donec prostratus succumberet arte maligni;
Ex me tunc priscæ processit causa ruinæ,
Dulcia quæ rudibus tradebam mala colonis.
5 En iterum mundo testor remeasse salutem,
Stipite de patulo dum penderet arbiter orbis
Et pœnas lueret soboles veneranda Tonantis.

LXXVII. FICULNEA

Quis prior in mundo deprompsit tegmina vestis
Aut quis clementer miserum protexit egenum?
Irrita non referam verbis nec frivola fingam.
Primitus in terra proprio de corpore peplum,
5 Ut fama fertur, produxi frondibus altis;
Carica me curvat, dum massis pabula præstat,
Sedulus agricola brumæ quas tempore mandit.

75. HORNET

Through sparkling air I sail on fourfold wings—
A frightful thing, with deep and murmurous voice;
And in a hollow stump I dwell in swarms,
Making sweet nutriment to feed my young—
5 Though human mouths are puckered by this food.
If any foe would break the pact of peace,
And grimly seek to stain with blood my home
Beneath its oaken roof, post-haste to war
I call my banded comrades, who in hordes
10 Raise tumult, thrusting deep their pikes, and rout
The enemy dismayed by savage darts;
For noisily upon the offending foe
They aim their shafts, in loathsome poison dipped.

76. APPLE-TREE

Happy at first was all the dawning world,
Till by the devil's wiles it prostrate fell.
I was the cause of that first ruinous fall,
Giving sweet apples to those untaught folk.
5 Lo, now I testify, salvation came
Again unto mankind when this world's King,
The holy Son of God the Thunderer,
Hung from a spreading tree to cleanse our sin.

77. FIG-TREE

Who first gave sheltering garments to the world,
Mercifully covering the destitute?
No empty words I speak, nor aught devise
Of silliness. Then first upon the earth,
5 So rumor runs, my high-hung leaves produced
A garment. Heavy with ripe figs I bend,
In clusters which the industrious farmer stores
To feed on in the time of wintry storms.

LXXVIII. Cupa Vinaria

En, plures debrians impendo pocula Bacchi,
Vinitor expressit quæ flavescentibus uvis
Pampinus et viridi genuit de palmite botris,
Nectare cauponis complens ex vite tabernam.
5 Sic mea turgescunt ad plenum viscera musto,
Et tamen inflatum non vexat crapula corpus,
Quamvis hoc nectar centenis hauserit urnis.
Proles sum terræ glescens in saltibus altis;
Materiam cuneis findit sed cultor agrestis
10 Pinos evertens altas et robora ferro.

LXXIX. Sol et Luna

Non nos Saturni genuit spurcissima proles
Iupiter, immensum fingunt quem carmina vatum,
Nec fuit in Delo mater Latona creatrix;
Cynthia non dicor nec frater Apollo vocatur,
5 Sed potius summi genuit regnator Olimpi,
Qui nunc in cælis excelsæ præsidet arci.
Dividimus mundum communi lege quadratum:
Nocturnos regimus cursus et frena dierum.
Ni soror et frater vaga sæcula iure gubernent,
10 Heu! chaos immensum clauderet cuncta latebris
Atraque nunc Erebi regnarent Tartara nigri.

LXXX. Calix Vitreus

De rimis lapidum profluxi flumine lento,
Dum frangant flammæ saxorum viscera dura

78. WINE-CASK

Many the men that I inebriate
By doling out full cups of heady wine
From golden clusters by the vintner pressed,
Born of the vine with green and tender shoots,
5 To stock with nectar every wayside inn.
Thus swelled and filled to bursting with new wine,
I feel intoxication not a whit,
Though from a hundred jars the must is poured.
The offspring of the earth am I, and grow
10 On lofty uplands; there the husbandman
Splits with his wedge the timber, laying low
Tall pines and towering oak-trees with the axe.

79. SUN AND MOON

Not Jupiter, old Saturn's cursed son,
Fathered us, he whom songs of poets call
The mighty one; Latona bore us not,
Feigned mother of us both, on Delos' isle.
5 I am not Cynthia, and my brother's name
Is not Apollo; rather is our sire
Ruler of highest heaven, who in the skies
Now reigns within his lofty citadel.
The foursquare world we share by mutual law:
10 We guide the coursing nights, rein in the days.
If I and my great brother by our rule
Directed not the wandering universe,
Alas, what boundless chaos would invest
All things in darkness, while black Tartarus,
15 The realm of night and death, would rule the world.

80. GLASS CUP

In sluggish stream I flowed from rifted rocks,
As flames broke up the stones, and fire applied

Et laxis ardor fornacis regnat habenis;
Nunc mihi forma capax glacieque simillima lucet.
5 Nempe volunt plures collum constringere dextra
Et pulchre digitis lubricum comprendere corpus;
Sed mentes muto, dum labris oscula trado
Dulcia compressis impendens basia buccis,
Atque pedum gressus titubantes sterno ruina.

LXXXI. Lucifer

Semper ego clarum præcedo lumine lumen
Signifer et Phœbi, lustrat qui limpidus orbem,
Per cælum gradiens obliquo tramite flector;
Eoas partes amo, dum iubar inde meabit
5 Finibus Indorum, cernunt qui lumina primi.
O felix olim servata lege Tonantis!
Heu! post hæc cecidi proterva mente superbus;
Ultio quapropter funestum perculit hostem.
Sex igitur comites mecum super æthera scandunt,
10 Gnarus quos poterit per biblos pandere lector.

LXXXII. Mustela

Discolor in curvis conversor quadripes antris
Pugnas exercens dira cum gente draconum.
Non ego dilecta turgesco prole mariti,
Nec fecunda viro sobolem sic edidit alvus,
5 Residuæ matres ut sumunt semina partus;
Quin magis ex aure prægnantur viscera fetu.
Si vero proles patitur discrimina mortis,
Dicor habere rudem componens arte medelam.

The unleashed ardor of the furnace-heat;
My form capacious now is clear as ice.
5 Yea, many long to hold me in their hand,
Fingering my slippery shape in dainty grasp;
But I befool their minds, the while I lay
Sweet kisses on their lips that press me close,
And urge their tottering footsteps to a fall.

81. Morning Star (Lucifer)

Bearing a light, I go before the light
Of morning, herald of the sun, who pours
A flood of glory on the world; I walk
A slanting way through heaven, and love the realm
5 Of dawn, when radiancy is shed athwart
The lands of India, first to see the day.
Once I was happy, when I kept the law
Of God the Thunderer. But, alas, I fell,
Wanton and proud of mind, and vengeance dropped
10 Upon my head—on me, the direful foe.
Hence, six companions mount the sky with me,
As readers wise in books may best explain.

82. Weasel

A parti-colored quadruped, I dwell
In rounded caverns, warring with the snakes,
A hateful tribe. I swell not with my young,
Dear children of my mate, nor does my womb,
5 Made fertile by the male, produce his race,
As other mothers do when they receive
The germ of offspring. Nay, my young at birth
Forth from my body at the ear I bring.
But if my children come to blows with death,
10 I brew by art, 't is said, rude remedies.

LXXXIII. Iuvencus

Arida spumosis dissolvens faucibus ora
Bis binis bibulus potum de fontibus hausi.
Vivens nam terræ glebas cum stirpibus imis
Nisu virtutis validæ disrumpo feraces;
5 At vero linquit dum spiritus algida membra,
Nexibus horrendis homines constringere possum.

LXXXIV. Scrofa Prægnans

Nunc mihi sunt oculi bis seni in corpore solo
Bis ternumque caput, sed cetera membra gubernant.
Nam gradior pedibus suffultus bis duodenis,
Sed decies novem sunt et sex corporis ungues,
5 Sinzigias numero pariter similabo pedestres.
Populus et taxus, viridi quoque fronde salicta
Sunt invisa mihi, sed fagos glandibus uncas,
Fructiferas itidem florenti vertice quercus
Diligo; sic nemorosa simul non spernitur ilex.

LXXXV. Cæcvs Natus

Iam referam verbis tibi, quod vix credere possis,
Cum constet verum fallant nec frivola mentem.
Nam dudum dederam soboli munuscula grata,
Tradere quæ numquam poterat mihi quislibet alter,
5 Dum Deus ex alto fraudaret munere claro,
In quo cunctorum gaudent præcordia dono.

LXXXVI. Aries

Sum namque armatus rugosis cornibus horrens,
Herbas arvorum buccis decerpo virentes,
Et tamen astrifero procedens agmine stipor,
Culmina cælorum quæ scandunt celsa catervis.
5 Turritas urbes capitis certamine quasso
Oppida murorum prosternens arcibus altis.
Induo mortales retorto stamine pepli;
Littera quindecima præstat, quod pars domus adsto.

83. STEER

My mouth I moisten through my foaming jaws,
When drink from twice two fountains I have gulped.
During my life, by huge and mighty strength
I break the fertile soil, and root up stumps;
5 But when the breath has left my icy limbs,
I then can bind strong men in fearful bonds.

84. PREGNANT SOW

Now in one body I have twice six eyes
And twice three heads, but all my other parts
Rule these.   Upborne on twice two feet I walk,
And yet my body's nails are ninety-six.
5 In number like a metric syzygy
I thus appear.   The poplar and the yew
And green-leaved willow-tree I hate, but love
The crooked beech-tree with its nuts, and oaks
With thick-crowned head that juicy acorns bear,
10 Nor do I scorn the holm-oak with its shade.

85. MAN BLIND FROM BIRTH

Now I shall tell what you can scarce believe,
Though true it is, not foolish trickery:
For once I gave my son a pleasing gift,
A gift which none could ever give to me,
5 Since God on high withheld this glorious boon,
In which all other men rejoice their hearts.

86. RAM

I am a frightful beast with crumpled horn;
I crop great mouthfuls of the growing grass,
Yet, as I go, I lead a starry host
Who mount in troops the peaks of lofty heaven.
5 By my head's battle-shock I shake tall towns,
Raze towered cities with their citadels.
I cover men with clothes of twisted thread.
If but the fifteenth letter stands before,
Part of a house at once I seem to be.

LXXXVII. Clipeus

De salicis trunco, pecoris quoque tergore raso
Componor patiens discrimina cruda duelli.
Semper ego proprio gestantis corpore corpus
Conservabo, viri vitam ne dempserit Orcus.
5 Quis tantos casus aut quis tam plurima leti
Suscipit in bello crudelis vulnera miles?

LXXXVIII. Basiliscus

Callidior cunctis aura vescentibus æthræ
Late per mundum dispersi semina mortis;
Unde horrenda seges diris succrevit aristis,
Quam metit ad scelera scortator falce maligna;
5 Cornigeri multum vereor certamina cervi.
Namque senescenti spoliabor pelle vetustus
Atque nova rursus fretus remanebo iuventa.

LXXXIX. Arca Libraria

Nunc mea divinis complentur viscera verbis
Totaque sacratos gestant præcordia biblos;
At tamen ex isdem nequeo cognoscere quicquam:
Infelix fato fraudabor munere tali,
5 Dum tollunt diræ librorum lumina Parcæ.

XC. Puerpera Geminas Enixa

Sunt mihi sex oculi, totidem simul auribus hausi,
Sed digitos decies senos in corpore gesto;
Ex quibus ecce quater denis de carne revulsis
Quinquies at tantum video remanere quaternos.

87. SHIELD

Of willow-wood am I and smooth ox-hide,
Enduring fateful shocks of bloody strife.
Ever with my own body I protect
The body of my bearer, lest grim death
5 Ravish the hero's life. In cruel war
What soldier undergoes such dire mischance,
Or can withstand so many deadly wounds?

88. SERPENT

Of all that breathe refreshing air of heaven,
I am most cunning, who through all the world
Flung wide the seeds of death, whence sprang a crop
Of grim and hideous grain; there with his scythe,
5 Measuring the yield to serve his evil plans,
Roams the Defiler. Never dare I fight
The stag with branching antlers. When old age
Falls on me, I cast off my worn-out skin,
And find my body staunch, my youth renewed.

89. BOOKCASE

My inwards overflow with words divine,
And sacred volumes crowd my vital parts,
But from them I can never learn one whit—
Unhappy creature, robbed of such a gift,
By my grim fate denied the light of books.

90. WOMAN IN LABOR WITH TWINS

Six eyes are mine; as many ears have I;
Fingers and toes twice thirty do I bear.
Of these, when forty from my flesh are torn,
Lo, then but twenty will remain to me.

XCI. PALMA

Omnipotens auctor, nutu qui cuncta creavit,
Mi dedit in mundo tam victrix nomen habendum.
Nomine nempe meo florescit gloria regum,
Martiribus necnon, dum vincunt prœlia mundi,
5 Edita cælestis prensant et præmia vitæ;
Frondigeris tegitur bellantum turma coronis
Et viridi ramo victor certamine miles.
In summo capitis densescit vertice vellus,
Ex quo multiplicis torquentur tegmina pepli;
10 Sic quoque mellifluis escarum pasco saginis
Nectare per populos tribuens alimenta ciborum.

XCII. FARUS EDITISSIMA

Rupibus in celsis, qua tundunt cærula cautes
Et salis undantes turgescunt æquore fluctus,
Machina me summis construxit molibus amplam,
Navigeros calles ut pandam classibus index.
5 Non maris æquoreos lustrabam remige campos
Nec ratibus pontum sulcabam tramite flexo
Et tamen immensis errantes fluctibus actos
Arcibus ex celsis signans ad litora duco
Flammiger imponens torres in turribus altis,
10 Ignea brumales dum condunt sidera nimbi.

XCIII. SCINTILLA

Quæ res in terris armatur robore tanto
Aut paribus fungi nitatur viribus audax?
Parva mihi primo constant exordia vitæ,
Sed gracilis grandes soleo prosternere leto,
5 Quod letum proprii gestant penetralia ventris.
Nam saltus nemorum densos pariterque frutecta

91. PALM

The Lord omnipotent, who by his will
Created all, named me 'victorious',
So to be called among the folk of earth.
Yea, by my name renown of kings glows bright,
5 And martyrs gain the prize of heavenly bliss,
When they have won the battles of the world;
The warrior bands are crowned with leafy crowns;
The soldier, victor in the fight, receives
The boon of my green bough. Upon my head
10 A thatch lies thick, whence fall in many folds
The robes that veil my form. And more than this,
Sweet food I give, and richly nourish all
Who feed upon my nectar-giving fruit.

92. TALL LIGHTHOUSE

On high crags, where the blue seas pound the reefs,
And briny billows swell the heaving flood,
Mechanic art has built me, great and high,
For ships a guiding finger to reveal
5 The open channel. Yet I never roam
The level sea in ships of many oars,
That cut a curving furrow through the deep;
But, pointing from my pinnacle, I lead
Those wanderers buffeted by mountain-waves
10 Safely to shore, lifting a fiery brand,
For high upon my tower a torch I set,
When wintry clouds conceal the flaming stars.

93. SPARK

What earthly thing is armed with might like mine,
Or boldly strives to use such force and strength?
Small was my life's beginning, but great things,
Though I am slender, low I lay in death,
5 A death my belly's inmost hollow hides.
For woodlands dense, groves, shrubs, and mountains tall,

Piniferosque simul montes cum molibus altos
Truxque rapaxque capaxque feroxque sub æthere spargo
Et minor existens gracili quam corpore scnifes,
10 Frigida dum genetrix dura generaret ab alvo
Primitus ex utero producens pignora gentis.

XCIV. EBULUS.

Sambucus, in silva putris dum fronde virescit,
Est mihi par foliis; nam glesco surculus arvis
Nigros bacarum portans in fronte corimbos.
Quem medici multum ruris per terga virentem,
5 Cum scabies morbi pulpas irrepserit ægras,
Lustrantes orbem crebro quæsisse feruntur:
Cladibus horrendæ, dum vexat viscera tabo,
Ne virus serpat, possum succurrere, lepræ,
Sic olidas hominum restaurans germine fibras.

XCV. SCILLA

Ecce, molosorum nomen mihi fata dederunt
(Argolicæ gentis sic promit lingua loquelis),
Ex quo me diræ fallebant carmina Circæ,
Quæ fontis liquidi maculabat flumina verbis:
5 Femora cum cruribus, suras cum poplite bino
Abstulit immiscens crudelis verba virago.
Pignora nunc pavidi referunt ululantia nautæ,
Tonsis dum trudunt classes et cærula findunt
Vastos verrentes fluctus grassante procella,
10 Palmula qua remis succurrit panda per undas,
Auscultare procul, quæ latrant inguina circum.
Sic me pellexit dudum Titania proles,
Ut merito vivam salsis in fluctibus exul.

Pine forests on their flanks, I murderously—
Savage and greedy, with capacious maw—
Lay waste, and scatter wide beneath the sky;
10 And yet my form was slighter than a gnat's
When first my icy mother brought me forth,
Producing offspring from her stony womb.

94. Dwarf Elder

The elder, growing green with stinking leaves
Within the wood, has foliage like my own;
I dwell in fields, a shrub, upon whose brow
Black berries hang in clusters.   Where I spring
5 Thick on the hillsides, doctors often come,
Roaming the wide earth through to seek me, when
Scabby disease has seized upon men's flesh;
For I can hinder poisonous leprosy,
Destroyer dread, from penetrating deep
10 To vex the organs, and, too, by my seeds,
Rank human bowels can restore to health.

95. Scylla

Lo, Fate has given me a canine name
(For thus the Argive speech expresses it)
Because dread Circe's songs enchanted me,
When by her words she stained the fountain's stream:
5 Weaving her magic spells, the heartless witch
Cruelly snatched away my legs and thighs
And buttocks.   Now the fearful mariners
Bring shrieking offerings to me, as with oars
They urge their ships, and cleave the azure sea—
10 Sweeping the billows in the raging blast,
While the curved oar-blade slides along the waves—
When they have heard far off those barking things
About my loins.   Thus was I long ago
Decoyed by Titan's daughter to endure
15 In briny seas an exile self-incurred.

XCVI. ELEFANS

Ferratas acies et denso milite turmas,
Bellandi miseros stimulat quos vana cupido,
Dum maculare student armis pia fœdera regni
Salpix et sorbet ventosis flatibus auras
5 Raucaque clangenti resultant classica sistro,
Cernere non pavidus didici trux murmura Martis.
Quamquam me turpem nascendi fecerit auctor,
Editus ex alvo dum sumpsi munera vitæ,
Ecce tamen morti successit gloria formæ,
10 Letifer in fibras dum finis serpat apertas;
Bratea non auri fulvis pretiosa metallis,
Quamvis gemmarum constent ornata lucernis,
Vincere, non quibunt falerarum floribus umquam.
Me flecti genibus fessum natura negavit
15 Poplite seu curvo palpebris tradere somnos,
Quin potius vitam compellor degere stando.

XCVII. Nox

Florida me genuit nigrantem corpore tellus
Et nil fecundum stereli de viscere promo,
Quamvis Eumenidum narrantes carmine vates
Tartaream partu testentur gignere prolem.
5 Nulla mihi constat certi substantia partus,
Sed modo quadratum complector cærula mundum.
Est inimica mihi, quæ cunctis constat amica,
Sæcula dum lustrat, lampas Titania Phœbi;
Diri latrones me semper amare solebant,
10 Quos gremio tectos nitor defendere fusco.

96. Elephant

Fearful, ferocious, I have learned to hear
The din of strife, to view grim battle-fronts
Bristling with steel, close ranks of warriors,
Poor wretches stung by fruitless lust for war,
5 Eager the kingdom's holy pacts to break
And violate by arms, while bugles blow,
Sucking in windy gusts of air, and hoarse
From blaring trumpet bursts the battle-call.
Though the Creator made me base of birth,
10 When, issuing from the womb, of life I took
The boon and burden, lo, when life is done,
I take on glorious beauty, as grim death,
The terminator, creeps into my veins:
No precious sheets of tawny gold, though decked
15 With glittering gems, my body can surpass,
Nor gorgeous trappings rich with broidered flowers.
Nature will never let me bend my knees,
Though I am weary, nor with crouching hams
Bring restful sleep upon my eyes; instead,
20 Standing perforce, I thus must pass my life.

97. Night

Black was I when from flowery earth I sprang,
And from my sterile womb no fertile thing
Can I produce, though poets in their songs,
Telling of the Eumenides, attest
5 That I once bred the race of Tartarus.
Such solid form as comes by natural birth
Is none of mine; but, azure-black of hue,
I hold the foursquare world in my embrace.
To me unfriendly is the Titan's torch,
10 To others friendly, since it lights the world.
Grim robbers ever love me, who defend
And in my dusky bosom hide them close.

Vergilium constat caram cecinisse sororem:
'Ingrediturque solo et caput inter nubila condit
Monstrum horrendum, ingens, cui quot sunt corpore plumæ,
Tot vigiles oculi subter, mirabile dictu,
15 Tot linguæ, totidem ora sonant, tot subrigit auris;
Nocte volat cæli medio terræque per umbras.'

XCVIII. ELLEBORUS

Ostriger en arvo vernabam frondibus hirtis
Conquilio similis: sic cocci murice rubro
Purpureus stillat sanguis de palmite guttis.
Exuvias vitæ mandenti tollere nolo
5 Mitia nec penitus spoliabunt mente venena;
Sed tamen insanum vexat dementia cordis,
Dum rotat in giro vecors vertigine membra.

IC. CAMELLUS

Consul eram quondam, Romanus miles equester
Arbiter imperio dum regni sceptra regebat;
Nunc onus horrendum reportant corpora gippi
Et premit immensum truculentæ sarcina molis.
5 Terreo cornipedum nunc velox agmen equorum,
Qui trepidi fugiunt mox quadripedante meatu,
Dum trucis aspectant immensos corporis artus.

C. CREATURA

Conditor, æternis fulcit qui sæcla columnis,
Rector regnorum, frenans et fulmina lege,
Pendula dum patuli vertuntur culmina cæli,
Me varium fecit, primo dum conderet orbem.

Thus Virgil of my sister sang: 'She walks
Upon the ground, and hides her head in clouds,
15 Strange, frightful, mighty, on whose body spring
Numberless feathers, and as many eyes
Lie watchful underneath, and, strange to tell,
As many mouths, as many tongues resound,
As many ears uplift; she flies midway
20 Between the earth and sky through shadowy night.'

98. HELLEBORE

Purple I bear, as in the fields I grow,
With hairy leaves, and like a mussel am:
With ruddy dye my berries drip like blood,
Red from my branches. No intent have I
5 To take the life of him who tastes of me,
Nor will my gentle poison quite despoil
His reason; yet a madness of the heart
Torments the fool who eats me, till he whirls
And turns in giddiness, a witless man.

99. CAMEL

A Roman knight and consul was I once,
Wielding the truncheon with a lordly hand;
But now a monstrous load my hump supports,
Galled by an irksome pack of killing weight.
5 Swift troops of hard-hoofed horses I affright,
Who flee in fear to see me lumbering by,
Four-legged, tall, and fierce to look upon.

100. NATURE

The Lord Creator, who supports the world
On everlasting columns, Guide of realms,
Bridling by law the lightning, while the sky,
Hanging in air, revolves its spacious dome,
5 When earth he stablished, made me manifold.

5 Pervigil excubiis: numquam dormire iuvabit,
   Sed tamen extemplo clauduntur lumina somno;
   Nam Deus ut propria mundum dicione gubernat,
   Sic ego complector sub cæli cardine cuncta.
   Segnior est nullus, quoniam me larbula terret,
10 Setigero rursus constans audacior apro;
   Nullus me superat cupiens vexilla triumphi
   Ni Deus, æthrali summus qui regnat in arce.
   Prorsus odorato ture flagrantior halans
   Olfactum ambrosiæ, necnon crescentia glebæ
15 Lilia purpureis possum conexa rosetis
   Vincere spirantis nardi dulcedine plena;
   Nunc olida cæni squalentis sorde putresco.
   Omnia, quæque polo sunt subter et axe reguntur,
   Dum pater arcitenens concessit, jure guberno;
20 Grossas et graciles rerum comprenso figuras.
   Altior, en, cælo rimor secreta Tonantis
   Et tamen inferior terris tetra Tartara cerno;
   Nam senior mundo præcessi tempora prisca,
   Ecce, tamen matris horno generabar ab alvo
25 Pulchrior auratis, dum fulget fibula, bullis,
   Horridior ramnis et spretis vilior algis.
   Latior, en, patulis terrarum finibus exto
   Et tamen in media concludor parte pugilli,
   Frigidior brumis necnon candente pruina,
30 Cum sim Vulcani flammis torrentibus ardens,
   Dulcior in palato quam lenti nectaris haustus
   Dirior et rursus quam glauca absinthia campi.
   Mando dapes mordax lurconum more Ciclopum,
   Cum possim iugiter sine victu vivere felix.
35 Plus pernix aquilis, Zephiri velocior alis,
   Necnon accipitre properantior, et tamen horrens
   Lumbricus et limax et tarda testudo palustris

I wake by night, nor ever love to sleep,
Yet straightway are my eyes in slumber closed;
Yea, as God sways creation by his word,
So all things under heaven do I control.
10 None is more cowardly, for the merest wraith
Affrights me, though I have a bolder heart
Than any bristly boar. Save God alone,
Who reigns supreme upon the hills of heaven,
None more desires the flags of victory.
15 In truth, I breathe ambrosial fragrance forth
More pungent than sweet frankincense, surpass,
By the full sweetness of exhaling nard,
Fresh lilies of the field and roses bright;
Yet now, with stinking, filthy nastiness,
20 I putrefy. All things beneath the sky,
All guided by its axis, I command,
So long as heaven-ruling God allows;
All shapes, both gross and graceful, I comprise.
Lo, higher than heaven, the secrets I explore
25 Of thundering God, yet, lower than the earth,
Gaze on foul hell; yea, older than the world,
I came before its infancy, and yet,
Behold, this year I left my mother's womb,
Lovelier than ornaments of tawny gold,
30 Uglier than buckthorn, viler than seaweed.
Lo, wider than the far-flung ends of earth
Extending, yet within the fist I lie;
Colder am I than winter and hoar frost,
Although I glow with Vulcan's flaming heat;
35 Sweeter than slow-dripped nectar to the taste,
More bitter than gray wormwood of the field;
Like gluttonous Cyclopes I gulp down food,
Though foodless I could always happy live.
Swifter than eagles or than Zephyr's wings,
40 And fleeter than the hawk am I, and yet
The cowering earthworm, snail, and tortoise slow,

Atque, fimi soboles sordentis, cantarus ater
Me dicto citius vincunt certamine cursus.
40 Sum gravior plumbo: scopulorum pondera vergo;
Sum levior pluma, cedit cui tippula limphæ;
Nam silici, densas quæ fudit viscere flammas,
Durior aut ferro, tostis sed mollior extis.
Cincinnos capitis nam gesto cacumine nullos,
45 Ornent qui frontem pompis et tempora setis,
Cum mihi cæsaries volitent de vertice crispæ,
Plus calamistratis se comunt quæ calamistro.
Pinguior, en, multo scrofarum axungia glesco,
Glandiferis iterum referunt dum corpora fagis
50 Atque saginata lætantur carne subulci;
Sed me dira famis macie torquebit egenam,
Pallida dum iugiter dapibus spoliabor opimis.
Limpida sum, fateor, Titanis clarior orbe,
Candidior nivibus, dum ningit vellera nimbus,
55 Carceris et multo tenebris obscurior atris
Atque latebrosis, ambit quas Tartarus, umbris.
Ut globus astrorum plasmor teres atque rotunda
Sperula seu pilæ necnon et forma cristalli;
Et versa vice protendor ceu Serica pensa
60 In gracilem porrecta panum seu stamina pepli.
Senis, ecce, plagis, latus qua panditur orbis,
Ulterior multo tendor, mirabile fatu;
Infra me suprave nihil per sæcula constat
Ni rerum genitor mundum sermone coercens.
65 Grandior in glaucis ballena fluctibus atra
Et minor exiguo, sulcat qui corpora, verme
Aut modico, Phœbi radiis qui vibrat, atomo;

Haunter of fens, and the black worm that springs
From ordure foul, faster than tongue can tell
Each could surpass me should we run a race.
45 Heavier than lead, I tip the scale, though rocks
Are weighed against me; lighter, too, than down
To which the very water-spider yields;
Harder than flint, that from itself strikes fire,
Or iron, but tenderer than roasted flesh.
50 Upon my head I wear no curly locks
That deck the brow with hirsute finery,
Although about my face floats waving hair
More crisp than ringlets made with curling-irons.
Much fatter, lo, am I than greasy sows
55 Dragging their bodies homeward from a feast
Of beech-mast to rejoice the swineherd's heart
With fattened flesh; but, sore in need and lean,
I bear dire hunger's torment, pale and wan,
Continually despoiled of sumptuous feasts.
60 Fair am I, I confess, more purely bright
Than Titan's orb, and whiter than the snow
When clouds let fleeces softly fall; more dark
Than dungeon's pitchy gloom, or those black shades
That fill up Tartarus. As smooth and round
65 Am I in form as astronomic globe,
Or ball, or crystal sphere; then, changing rôles,
I stretch out formless, like thin Chinese silk,
Spun to a gauzy fabric or rich robe.
Much farther, wonderful to tell, I reach
70 Than those six zones that mark the world's extent;
Below me or above me naught exists
In Nature save the Father of all things,
Whose word commands the world. I greater am
Than the black whale upon the gray-green waves,
75 Or smaller than the little worm which bores
Through corpses, smaller than the tiny mote
Trembling in Phœbus' rays. Through grassy fields

Centenis pedibus gradior per gramina ruris
Et penitus numquam per terram pergo pedester.
70 Sic mea prudentes superat sapientia sofos,
Nec tamen in biblis docuit me littera dives
Aut umquam quivi, quid constet sillaba, nosse.
Siccior æstivo torrentis caumate solis,
Rore madens iterum plus uda flumine fontis;
75 Salsior et multo tumidi quam marmora ponti
Et gelidis terræ limphis insulsior erro,
Multiplici specie cunctorum compta colorum,
Ex quibus ornatur præsentis machina mundi,
Lurida cum toto nunc sim fraudata colore.
80 Auscultate mei credentes famina verbi,
Pandere quæ poterit gnarus vix ore magister
Et tamen infitians non retur frivola lector!
Sciscitor inflatos, fungar quo nomine, sofos.

EXPLICIUNT ENIGMATA

I walk upon a hundred feet, and yet
I truly never go on foot at all.
80 Thus does my wisdom far surpass the lore
Of wise philosophers; yet was I taught
By no rich-lettered books, nor ever learned
The rhyme and reason of a syllable.
Drier than summer blazing from the sun,
85 Yet am I dripping dew, more wet than brooks
That rise from welling springs; and far more salt
Than the broad bosom of the heaving sea,
But fresher than cool inland streams I flow.
Adorned with all the lovely varied hues
90 That beautify the structure of this world,
Yet am I robbed of all fair coloring.
  Hear and believe my words, scarce to be cleared
By any schoolman skilled in speech; and yet
That reader who denies them, at the end
95 Will think them far from trifling! Now I ask
Puffed-up philosophers what name I bear.

HERE END THE RIDDLES

NOTES*

Prologue. Observe the acrostic and telestich, 'Aldhelmus cecinit millenis versibus odas.' Ehwald points out that this verse is to be compared with line 2895 of the *Carmen de Virginitate:* 'Dum decies denis modulantur milibus odas,' and that the prologue of the riddles has much in common with the prologue of that poem. There also, Aldhelm indulges in acrostic and telestich; the first letters reading down give the same verse as the last letters reading up: 'Metrica tirones nunc promant carmina castos,' the last line of the prologue being the acrostic verse (which is also the first line) read backwards: 'Sotsac animrac tnamorp cnun senorit acirtem.' In spite of the difficulty involved in this display of skill, the verses proceed with a fair fluency. Since the riddles contain only 800 verses, Aldhelm here, as elsewhere, is using 'thousand' merely as a round number.

4(4) *Vehemoth.* Job 40. 15. Ehwald quotes Gregory, *Moral.* 32. 10. 16: 'Quem sub Behemoth nomine nisi antiquum hostem insinuat?'

20(25) *cephal.* Coined by Aldhelm from κεφαλή. He uses it also *Carm. de Virg.* 1016.

21(26) *psalmista.* Ps. 109. 3.

30(37) *belliger . . . Iob.* 'Belliger est Iob, quoniam "certamina spiritualia sustinuerat."' Ehwald. Note the limping metre of this line—an infrequent occurrence with Aldhelm; cf. 25. 5; 79. 10; 100. 37.

1. **Earth.** An interesting unconscious parallel to this is a riddle on the plough, from an eighteenth-century chap-book (John Ashton, *Chap-books of the Eighteenth Century,* p. 301):

> To ease men of their care
> I do both rend and tear
> Their mother's bowels still;
> Yet tho' I do,
> There are but few
> That seem to take it ill.

It is noticeable that neither this riddler nor Aldhelm allows Earth's own offspring to do the tearing.

4. **Nature (Natural Force).** Cf. 100, *Creatura,* which I also translate 'Nature.' In *Natura,* Aldhelm points out merely the stupendously regulated force of nature; in *Creatura,* he touches on

* Figures in parentheses refer to lines of the translation.

many other qualities, notably those which illustrate the innate paradox of nature.

6. Moon. Cf. 79 for other attributes of the moon.

7. Fate. Despite his manifest love of the pagan poets, and his delight in mythology, Aldhelm never lets us forget that he is writing for the glory of Christianity. Cf. 57. 1, and 79.

2(2) Virgil, *Aen.* 12. 677.

8. Pleiades. Ehwald quotes Isidore (*Orig.* 3. 70. 13): 'Pliades a pluralitate dictæ; . . . sunt autem stellæ septem ante genua tauri, ex quibus sex videntur, nam latet una. Has Latini vergilias dicunt a temporis significatione, quod est ver, quando exoriuntur.'

9. Diamond. This idea of the potency of goat's blood is at least as old as Pliny.

11. Bellows. Cf. Symphosius 72, and the Old English *Riddle 38(37)*.

12. Silkworm. The introduction of broom as the food of this creature apparently indicates that Aldhelm, having observed caterpillars feeding on that plant and spinning cocoons of silk, identifies them with the true, mulberry-eating silkworm (*bombyx*), of which he has seen only the refined product. It is possible, also, that Aldhelm is himself aware of the distinction, but that the text of the title is at fault. At any rate, Aldhelm's caterpillar is probably that of some kind of Saturnia moth—Manitius (*Gesch. der Lat. Lit. des Mittelalters* 1. 138) conjectures '*Saturnia carpini* (or *spini?*).' See 12, and 100. 59 (67) for other references to silk and the silkworm.

13. Organ. Aldhelm's frequent references to music and musical instruments remind us of the tradition that he composed and sang songs in the vernacular in order to attract an audience for his sermons. In Cook's 'The Old English Andreas and Bishop Acca of Hexham' (*Trans. Conn. Acad. of Arts and Sciences* 26. 328) he has this note: ' "Aldhelm has many references to music and musical instruments; thus to organs, for example: ed. Ehwald 356. 69-72; 424. 1716-7; 466. 2786-9; 510. 4-6; 189. 15-6; 292. 16 ff.; cf. Ehwald's index under *musica, melodia, armonia,* etc." Faritius, his first biographer, writes of Aldhelm (chap. 1): "Musicæ autem artis omnia instrumenta, quæ fidibus vel fistulis aut aliis varietatibus melodiæ fieri possunt, et memoria tenuit et in quotidiano usu habuit." '

14. Peacock. This belief in the non-putrefying quality of the peacock's flesh is old and wide-spread.

16. Flying-fish. *Loligo* (not *luligo*, as here) is properly a kind of cuttle-fish, and the word is so used by Pliny, who, however, introduces the legendary detail that it 'flies, lifting itself out of the water, darting like an arrow, as do also the scallops' (*Nat. Hist.* 9. 45).

Again (18. 87), he cites the flying of the *loligo* as a sign of storm, and later introduces more confusion by linking it with the *milvago* ('gurnard', a species of spiny-headed fish, which, while not the true flying-fish, leaps out of the water in much the same manner): 'The gurnard is often seen flying quite out of the water. . . . The cuttle-fish (*loligo*), too, [Trebius Niger] reports, flies out of the water in such numbers as to sink ships' (*Nat. Hist.* 32. 6). This last legend still survives in the modern tales of giant octopuses. That the *loligo* is here considered a fish is shown both by the sense of the riddle, and by the various glosses (*piscis volans,* etc.). Perhaps Aldhelm saw flying-fish in the Mediterranean.

17. Purple-mussel. Cf. 98.

18. Ant-lion. The word *myrmicoleon* is found as a misread-ing in Job 4. 11; but almost anywhere that ants abound, the insect Aldhelm describes may be found building its ingenious trap.

22. Nightingale. 'Ακαλανθίς is properly the goldfinch, but, as can be seen both from the details of this riddle, and from 68. 7, where he identifies it with the Latin *luscinia,* Aldhelm understands the word as 'nightingale'.

24. Dragon-stone. See Pliny, *Nat. Hist.* 37. 158.

25. Magnet. The demagnetizing power of *adamas* is noted by Pliny and other writers, but why Aldhelm specifies *adamas Cypri,* I can not say. In 9, *adamas* is 'diamond', and is so used by Pliny in the same connection as here (*Nat. Hist.* 20. 1).

5 *potentia.* Note the false quantity; cf. *Præfatio* 30; 79. 10; 100. 37.

26. Cock. The crowing cock is a familiar figure in Latin hymns. It is rather surprising that Aldhelm makes no mention of St. Peter in this riddle, though that may be what he means by saying that the cock enjoys 'a name of wide repute'.

27. Whetstone. Cf. 21.

28. Minotaur. The Minotaur, a creature half man, half bull, was the issue of Pasiphaë, the wife of King Minos of Crete, and a bull; hence his hybrid name.

29. Water.

3(3-4) *acus . . . rumpit.* Ehwald's note reads: 'Naves, quas aqua tulit, ad scopulum acutum appulsæ naufragium faciunt.' I can not agree with this interpretation; this riddle has nothing to do with either the fragility or the strength of ships. *Gesta-mina* is here not the thing carried (the original and usual mean-ing), but the carrier, a not infrequent use of the word, for which see the examples in Harpers' Dictionary, e. g., '*lento gestamine vilis aselli,* Sedul. 4, 297.' (It is perhaps a mere coïncidence that 63. 7 is a line quoted bodily from Sedulius.) Any other rendering destroys the sense and symmetry of the passage, in which Water is showing the paradox of its nature, its strength and weakness; otherwise, the riddle contains no expression of the dominant characteristic of water—its fluidity.

30. Alphabet. Aldhelm (following Isidore, *Orig.* 1. 4. 10) means that *h, k, q, x, y, z* are not native Latin letters: that leaves seventeen in the Latin alphabet, since *w* is a modern invention, and *u=v* and *j=i.* Properly speaking, there would be only sixteen, since *c* and *g* were originally the same letter.

3(3-4). Cf. 32.
4(4-5). Cf. 59.
5(6). The 'three brothers' are the thumb, forefinger, and middle finger—those which hold the pen. Cf. 74. 8(9), where the same fingers are shown manipulating a sling.
6-7(7-8). Cf. 89.

32. Writing-tablets. Aldhelm has in mind waxed wooden tablets for temporary writing, such as were used by the Romans. The writing was done by means of a metal stylus, and erasures were made by smoothing down the wax with the flattened top of the same instrument. Line 3, however, is puzzling. In the first place, since both nouns are neuter plurals, it may be rendered either 'shoes gave me my hard backs,' or 'tough hides gave me my shoes.' The juxtaposition of *calciamenta* and *mihi* seems to favor the latter, but I can not visualize the tablets' shoes. The former, which I have accepted for the translation, would seem to mean that the tablets are backed in some way with leather, perhaps somewhat as a book is bound in half leather, though the *pugillares* of classical times seem not to have been so made. If this interpretation is correct, the use of 'shoes' for 'leather', and the employment of the ambiguous *tergora,* apparently indicate that Aldhelm is purposely bewildering his readers.

4(3-4). Cf. 30.
8(8-9). Aldhelm clearly knows something of the effects of war on civilization. Note also that he regards as the principal office of writing the dissemination of the Gospel. Cf. 59.

33. Cuirass.

3(4) *Seres . . . vermes.* Cf. 12, and 100. 59(67).

34. Locust. See Exodus 10. 5, 14 ff. 'I have put lines 6 and 7

before line 4, because of the sense and the grammatical construction.'—
Ehwald.

35. Night-raven. See Ps. 102. 6, where the Vulgate reads:
'Similis factus sum pelicano solitudinis: factus sum sicut nycticorax
in domicilio,' but the Authorized Version has: 'I am like a pelican
of the wilderness: I am like an owl of the desert.' The difference
of course lies in the variant readings of the text of the original.
Aldhelm evidently connects the first part of the name with *nox,*
following Isidore, *Orig.* 12. 7. 41.

36. Gadfly. Isidore says (*Orig.* 12. 8. 14) that *cyniphes* were the
flies (*muscæ minutissimæ*) which infested Egypt in the third plague.
The third plague (Exodus 8), that of *cyniphes* in the Vulgate, is
called the plague of lice in both the Authorized and American
Revised Versions, and the latter adds the note: 'Or, *sand flies;* or,
fleas.' The fourth plague is that of the *muscæ* in the Vulgate, trans-
lated 'flies' in the English versions. Apparently Isidore guessed at
the meaning of *cyniphes.*

37. Crab.

1(1). *Nepa* really means 'scorpion', not 'crab.' 4-5 refers to
the sign of the zodiac.
6(6). According to Isidore (*Orig.* 12. 6. 51), the crab, wait-
ing until the oyster opens its shell, casts in a stone to prevent
its closing, and then dines upon the flesh within.

38. Water-spider. Cf. 100. 41(47). I have often seen a species
of *tippula,* popularly called 'water-boatman,' which glides very rapidly
over the water on four legs, each shod with what appears to be a tiny
pontoon. The word *suffulta* is well chosen: in some I have recently
seen, the legs raised the body so high above the water—perhaps a
quarter of an inch—that the creature's reflection was easily visible
beneath it.

39. Lion. Ehwald quotes Isidore (*Orig.* 12. 2. 3): 'Leo autem
Græce, Latine rex interpretatur;' and (*ibid.* 12. 2. 5): 'Cum dormi-
erint, vigilant oculi.'

41. Pillow.

4-5(4-5) *caput . . . capitis.* Ehwald's note is: 'v. 4 caput
est indumentum plumarum [the bag of ticking?], v. 5 hominis
incumbentis.'

42. Ostrich.

5(5-6). 'The contents [of ostrich eggs], equal to those of
some two dozen hens' eggs, are used for food by the natives,
the shells forming convenient pots for water and so forth' (*Cam-
bridge Natural History* 9. 29).

45. Spindle. This is obviously the simplest form of spindle, to be used in the right hand, with the distaff held under the left elbow. The order of lines is not altogether satisfactory in this riddle. In Giles' text, line 6 follows line 4, and, indeed perhaps thus betters the sense, though that order would separate lines 3 and 4, which apparently belong together. But Ehwald here restores the order of the codices, and hence I follow him. The numbering of his text shows his rearrangement.

3(3) *molam.* This word (not in the dictionaries) is explained by Isidore (*Orig.* 20. 8. 6) : 'Mola a rotunditate sui vocata, ut mala pomorum, sic et Græci;' it means the clump of flax held on the distaff, from which the thread is spun. This line is virtually repeated in *Carmina de Virginitate* 1464: 'Quod [fusum] vehit in collo tereti vertigine molam.'

46. Nettle. This is an adaptation of Symphosius' riddle (44) on the onion :

> Mordeo mordentes, ultro non mordeo quemquam;
> Sed sunt mordentum multi mordere parati;
> Nemo timet morsum, dentes quia non habeo ullos.

For other examples of this play on words, see Manitius, *Gesch. der Lat. Lit. des Mittelalters* 1. 206.

47. Swallow. The question of how the swallow spends the winter has been a matter of concern to naturalists until recent times. Goldsmith, in his *Animated Nature* (1774), discusses the matter at length, citing opinions and experiments of those who thought variously that the bird migrated, hibernated on dry land, or passed the winter under water. Aldhelm apparently is of the opinion that it simply seeks some secluded place (*umbrosas latebras*) to winter in.

7-9(7-10). Pliny tells us of this plant (*Chelidonium;* χελιδών is the Greek for 'swallow') : 'Chelidonium visui saluberrimam hirundines monstravere, vexatis pullorum oculis illa medentes' (*Nat. Hist.* 8. 41) ; and Isidore (*Orig.* 17. 9. 36) repeats the account.

48. Sphere of the Heavens. *Vertico = vertigo,* properly 'a whirling about', but the text clearly indicates the particular sense here. Isidore tells us (*Orig.* 3. 35) that the speed of the heavens would destroy the world, if it were not that the stars move in the opposite direction, and thus impede the motion.

9(10). The *septem sidera* are the 'planets', including the sun and moon, for which see Proclus' commentary on Plato's *Alcibiades;* cf. 81. 9(11).

49. Cauldron. Aldhelm revels in natural paradoxes, as witness 100.

1(1). Ehwald quotes Isidore (*Orig.* 20. 8. 4) : 'Lebetes aënei sunt Græco sermone vocati; sunt ollæ minores in usum coquendi paratæ.'

50. Milfoil (Yarrow). Cf. Pliny (*Nat Hist.* 24. 95) : 'Myriophyllon, quod nostri millefolium vocant, caulis est tener, similis fœniculo, plurimis foliis : unde et nomen accepit. Nascitur in palustribus, magnifici usus ad vulnera.'

51. Heliotrope. Cf. Pliny (*Nat. Hist.* 2. 41) : 'Miretur hoc, qui non observet cotidiano experimento, herbam unam, quæ vocatur heliotropium, abeuntem solem intueri semper, omnibusque horis cum eo verti, vel nubilo obumbrante;' and (*Nat. Hist.* 22, 29) : 'Heliotropii miraculum sæpius diximus, cum sole se circumagentis, etiam nubilo die : tantus sideris amor est : noctu velut desiderio contrahi cæruleum florem.' Pliny nowhere else seems to mention the color of the blossom. Aldhelm's flower is yellow; is he thinking of the ordinary yellow sunflower? Cf. also Isidore, *Orig.* 17. 8. 37.

52. Candle.

4(5). The candle is made of yellow bee's wax.

53. Great Bear. Aldhelm here uses *Arcturus* for *Arctus*, as does Isidore (*De Nat. Rerum* 26. 3).—EHWALD.

6(9). Cf. *De Metris*, chap. 3 (ed. Ehwald, p. 72) : 'Nam arcturus Ripheis prælatus montibus, qui boreo aquilonalis poli cardine volvitur, qua Scithica regna horrendum incolunt barbariem, septiformi temonis et plaustri sidere signatur'; and Virgil, *Georg.* 240-241 :
Mundus, ut ad Scythiam Rhipæasque arduus arces Consurgit.

54. Double Cooking-vessel. Apparently something like a modern chafing-dish. I translate Ehwald's note: 'Aldhelm seems to me to be describing a cooking-vessel, not a utensil connected with sacrifice, as Dietrich and Prehn think: it is called double because the upper part holds water, and the lower fire or coals; the gloss in the Codex Cottonianus adds: "[A kind of pot] which pirates are wont to have on board ship." '

55. Ciborium. Obviously this is not the chrismatory (receptacle for the anointing oils) as the title states, nor the pyx, which is not counted a sacred vessel. Since it contains the symbols of Christ's redeeming act (cf. Aldhelm's *Carmina Ecclesiastica* 3. 70-76; ed. Ehwald, p. 18), it is probably the ciborium (sometimes confused with the pyx, though the latter holds only the bread of the sacrament). The *NED.* definition reads: 'Applied [by a mistaken derivation from *cibus*] to a receptacle for the reservation of the Eucharist. Of different forms; sometimes suspended from the roof or ciborium (sense I [a canopy erected over the high-altar]), sometimes having the form of a temple or tabernacle, sometimes of a cup with an arched cover;' and the examples which follow show that the vessel was elaborately ornamented with gold and jewels—*e. g.,* Evelyn, *Diary* (ed. 1827) 2. 33: 'I stept into ye Jesuites, who had this high day exposed their ciborium, made all of solid gold and imagerie.' Hence it is plain that Aldhelm is writing with his eye on the object, and that line 9 is not metaphoric, but refers directly to the form of the cabinet. Cf. the Old English *Riddle 49(48).*

56. Beaver.

6-8(7-9). Castoreum, a substance found in two inguinal sacs of the beaver, was once much used in medicine. Castor-oil (though the word may have a different derivation) is perhaps so called because it partially replaced castoreum for medical purposes.

57. Eagle.

1(1-2). Cf. Virgil, *Aen.* 5. 254.
6(7)ff. Cf. Ps. 103. 5.

For the uncomplimentary use of *infausti* (1) cf. 7, and note; 79.

58. Evening Star (Vesper). Cf. 81, *Lucifer,* the morning star.

6(7-8). The evening star is contemplating the downfall of Lucifer (cf. Isa. 14) as something not unlikely to happen to itself.

59. Pen. Cf. 30. I do not know why Aldhelm's pen should be taken from the pelican. That bird is usually dealt with under the aspect of the 'life-giving pelican'.

60. Unicorn. Isidore (*Orig.* 12. 2. 12 ff.) recounts these qualities of the unicorn. Pliny, in his description (*Nat. Hist.* 8. 31), expressly says: 'Hanc feram vivam negant capi.'

61. Dagger. Once more Aldhelm has the object before him. His dagger has a handle of horn, and is enclosed in a sheath of wood, covered with leather.

63. Raven. Cf. Genesis 8. 6-7.

7 is Sedulius 1. 175. The point is that the raven, having failed the good cause during the flood, later reëstablished its reputation by feeding Elijah in the wilderness.

8-9(9-11). Isidore gives this detail (*Orig.* 12. 7. 43). Pinfeathers do blacken beneath the skin, just as a beard shows blue on the face.

10(11-12). *Corbus—c=orbus,* 'childless'.

64. Dove. Cf. Genesis 8. 8-12.

6(7). Ehwald quotes Isidore (*Orig.* 7. 3. 22) : 'Hæc enim avis corporaliter ipso felle caret, habens tantum innocentiam et amorem.'

65. Cat.

9(11). *Muriceps*='catcher of mice', the 'gens exoso'.

67. Sieve. Cf. 70, where Aldhelm again uses the metaphor of frost and snow for flour. Ehwald restores the order of lines of the codices, as shown by his numbering.

68. Trumpet.

8(9). *acalantida.* Cf. 22, and note.

69. Yew-tree.

5. *Reorum* is surprising here. The yew-tree is *reus,* 'a guilty thing', but the Fates, who determine the natures of things, are responsible.

70. Bannock. Cf. 67. A bannock is a flat, round cake of almost any kind of flour, and was the common form of bread in Aldhelm's time. The Latin word, *tortella,* used here, is preserved in the Spanish *tortilla,* which is still a thin, flat, round cake, baked on hot stones or a griddle.

71. Fish.

3(3-4) involves a contradiction of riddle 16, *Flying-fish.*

5(6) refers to the sign of the zodiac.

72. Colossus. This is the Colossus of Rhodes, one of the ancient seven wonders of the world. According to our information, it was a huge lighthouse in the form of a man standing astride the entrance to the harbor. In his uplifted left hand he held a torch, and in his right hand, hanging at his side, a dart.

73. Spring of Water.

4-5(5-6). Is this another indication of Aldhelm's interest in the world of insects (cf. 12, 18, 20, 34, 36, 38, 43, 75), or is it merely a reference to the idea that all life originally sprang from water (cf. 29. 4-5)?

74. Sling. Cf. 1 Samuel 17.

75. Hornet.

1(1) *binis remigo pennis.* 'Since hornets have four wings, either Aldhelm is describing falsely a creature which he must have been able to see every day, or else we should read *bis binis.*'—EHWALD. This I have done.

76. Apple-tree. Cf. Genesis 3.

4(4) *dulcia . . . mala. Mala* may here be meant for a paradoxical pun, although the quantity would not permit the meaning 'evil'; Aldhelm occasionally—though remarkably seldom—admits a false quantity. Cf. *Præfatio* 30; 25. 5; 79. 10; 100. 37.

5(5). Being a tree, the subject of this riddle, in common with all trees, may stand for the rood.

77. Fig-tree. Cf. Genesis 3. 7.

7(8) *brumæ . . . tempore.* Aldhelm must have seen figs, both fresh and dried, in Italy.

79. Sun and Moon. Cf. 6.

1(1) *spurcissima.* This epithet saves Aldhelm's reputation as a Christian, as do the emphatic denials of ancient mythology in this riddle. Cf. 7 and 57.

10 *clauderet.* Notice that, since the metre requires *claudēret,* Aldhelm has either confused *claudĕre,* 'to close', with *claudēre,* 'to limp', or else is admitting a false quantity; cf. *Præfatio* 30; 25. 5; 100. 37.

81. Lucifer (Morning Star). Cf. 58, and Prologue 23(29).

9(11). Cf. 48. 9(10), and note.

82. Weasel. The common form of the legend (cf. Isidore, *Orig.* 12. 3. 3, who rejects it) is that the weasel conceives at the mouth (*ex ore*). Possibly *ore* should here be read for *aure.*

83. Steer. Cf. the Old English *Riddle 39(38).*

2(2) *bis binis . . . fontibus.* The teats of the cow.

3-4(3-4). The ox drawing the plough.

5-6(5-6). The hide cut into leather thongs.

84. Pregnant Sow. Cf. 90.

5(5) *sinzigias . . . pedestres.* Aldhelm says (*De Metris,* chap. 112; ed. Ehwald, p. 150): 'Nam de quinque sillabis .XXXII. pedes formantur, de sex sillabis .LXIV. sinzigiæ reciproca varietate nascuntur;' that is, a foot of more than five syllables is no longer a foot, but a syzygy. Hence, since the sow has a litter of five, counting herself she is in number equal to the number of syllables in a 'metric syzygy'. As for the spelling, *sinzigias,* Aldhelm often uses *i* for *y,* and by the *n* merely shows us that he knows the derivation of the first syllable.

85. Man Blind from Birth. The 'gift' is, of course, sight, which the man never received from his parents, but which he has been able to give to his offspring.

86. Ram. Aldhelm refers in succession to the animal, the sign of the zodiac, the battering-ram, wool, and finally, by prefixing *p*, turns *aries* into *paries*, 'wall'. In 63, he lops off a letter to form a word.

88. Serpent.

1(1). Cf. Vulg. Genesis 3. 1: 'Sed et serpens erat callidior cunctis animalibus terræ quæ fecerat Dominus Deus.'

5(6-7). Pliny tells us (*Nat. Hist.* 8. 20; 22. 37) of the enmity between stags and serpents.

6-7(7-9). Cf. 57.

89. Bookcase. Cf. 30.

90. Woman in Labor with Twins. This is merely a dull repetition of the idea of 84.

92. Tall Lighthouse. One of the most charming of the riddles. Wildman, who translates it, p. 86, suggests that there may in Aldhelm's day have been some kind of a lighthouse on St. Alban's Head (originally St. Aldhelm's Head), and that Aldhelm may have had it in mind when he wrote this riddle.

93. Spark. Cf. 44, where, too, we have the contrast between the cold mother (flint) and her offspring, and the mystery of great might arising from a small beginning.

94. Dwarf Elder. *Sambucus Ebulus,* of the Honeysuckle Family; known also as Danewort. See Pliny, *Nat. Hist.* 26. 49, 73, for various medical uses of the *Ebulus.*

95. Scylla. Aldhelm derives *Scylla* from the Greek σκύλαξ, 'whelp'. He is certainly following Ovid here (*Met.* 14. 40-67). Glaucus, having been refused by Scylla on account of his uncouth appearance, gets Circe to weave a spell against her, and Circe consents, more from jealously than from any other motive. Throwing magic poisons into a pool where Scylla is wont to bathe, she causes Scylla's body, from the waist down, to become a mass of barking dogs' heads, 'such as a Cerberus might have. She stands on ravening dogs, and her docked loins and her belly are enclosed in a circle of beastly forms.' Her eating of sailors is referred to in Ovid, and told of more fully in the Odyssey, and elsewhere.

96. Elephant. Cf. 32. There is something rather impressive here in this tirade of Aldhelm against war; he is apparently no militarist.

9-13(12-16). Aldhelm must have seen some beautiful objects made of ivory, to wax thus eloquent.

14-16(18-20). See Brehms, *Tierleben* 33. 15.

97. Night.

3-4(3-5). So Virgil, *Aen.* 12. 846.

12-16(13-20). Virgil, *Aen.* 4. 177, 181-184, the description of Rumor.

98. Hellebore.

1-3(1-4). *Cf.* 17; here we have another source of dye. See Virgil, *Georg.* 3. 451; Horace, *Ep.* 2. 2. 137; Lenz, *Botanik der Alten Griechen und Römer;* Pliny, *Nat. Hist.* 25. 21, 94.

99. Camel.

1(1). *Camellus* (properly *camelus*) is a bad pun on *Camillus*, the famous consul who captured Veii. Symphosius is fond of punning on a man's name. His riddle on the bull (32) is a play on the name of Statilius Taurus, and that on the mouse (25) puns on the name of Publius Decius Mus:

Parva mihi domus est, sed ianua semper aperta;
Exiguo sumptu furtiva vivo rapina;
Quod mihi nomen inest, Romæ quoque consul habebo.

Perhaps Symphosius had used all the good ones, leaving Aldhelm none better than *Camillus-Camellus.*

3 *gippi*=*gibbi,* 'a hump'.

100. Nature. Cf. the Old English *Riddle 41(40)* and *Riddle 67(66).* Aldhelm is here describing creation in its entirety: both the concrete created form, and the creative power which both comprehends and pervades everything. The essence of the idea of the riddle is therefore paradox, for that is the only way in which Aldhelm can express what is at once infinitely large and infinitely small—infinite in every conceivable way. Reflections of many of the other riddles will be found in this one.

9 *larbula*=*larvula.*

37. Note the faulty metre; cf. *Præfatio* 30; 25. 5; 79. 10.

41(47). See 38.

61(70) *senis* . . . *plagis.* I do not know whence Aldhelm gets this opinion about *six* zones, for he differs here from both Isidore and Bede, who say that the world is divided into five zones.

82(94-95). This line is incomprehensible unless we imagine Aldhelm as indulging in irony. Since these riddles, and *Creatura* particularly, deal with Christian truths, the reader who denies them will be denying truth, and so will be damned; then he will find that the riddles he once despised were not trifling—nor to be trifled with.

Date Due

[redacted]

DEC 01 2003			

PRINTED IN U.S.A. CAT. NO. 24 161 BRODART